BECOMING QUEEN BEE

PURPOSE THROUGH BRAVERY

QUEEN BEE™

BY

ELIN WIBELL AND MARIE FALKENBERG

SW
GLOBAL
PUBLISHING

Published by SW Global Publishing

SW Global Publishing (Australia)

Brisbane, Australia

www.swglobalpublishing.com

ISBN: 978-0-6452371-1-5

Edited and proofread by
Samantha Worthington

Front Cover Design and Typeset by Vince Embry Rivera

Our journey together started in 2019, after our class reunion. We were happy to see each other after many years without contact. Over dinner in Southern Spain, we realized how we both have gone through transitions to explore what life really meant to us. We felt an urge to share our learnings with you.

We both wanted to avoid one of the most common regrets of all which is not to live true to yourself. So many dreams go unfulfilled due to choices made or not made.

This book contains some learnings and methods to take control of your life. To ensure you focus on the things you are meant to. It is an easy task. You just need to put down some effort to define what it is you want.

We started to merge our thoughts when a pandemic hit and forced us into isolation. Our book was written during the Coronavirus quarantine but would take us to all parts of the world through the stories of the people we interviewed.

While listening to the stories of transformation and bravery, we realized they would serve as an inspiration and support for others to consider taking the leap themselves. A female empowerment idea rose. A network to support others to find their purpose through bravery. We decided to call it Queen Bee™

QUEEN BEE™

The French Emperor Napoleon Bonaparte was not only a great military leader but a driving force for revolutionary change. His most important symbol of the power and prestige of his empire was the honeybee. However, what was not recognized during this time was the underlying fact that the Queen Bee is the one in charge of the colony.

We found this to be a suitable name. "Queen Bee Syndrome" has been synonymous with a woman who puts other females down, so that she can retain her position as the "Queen Bee". We need to prove that this era is gone and change that concept. Let's work together, because together we are stronger.

Join Us
www.queenbeecolony.com

This book will guide you to take control of your life.

We dedicate it to you fantastic women.

ABOUT THE AUTHORS

Elin Wibell - After more than a decade at Corporate Communications working with corporate visions and purposes, I was surprised by the notion that the same effort was not applied to personal life. In 2015, I left my steady job and the 18,000 employee FMCG to embark on a journey to explore my personal purpose.

This brought me on a life-changing exploration to Asia, to NGO work, to app development. Writing this book, six years later I am currently based in southern Europe where I advise on corporate social responsibility. The 3-step Becoming Queen Bee™ Exercise is a replica of the method I used when planning my own transformation. I hope it will serve as a tool for you to become the best version of yourself.

Marie Falkenberg - During my mid-30s, I felt stuck in a situation in which I wasn't fully happy. I had always done what good girls do; study, get a job, help friends and family, and prioritize others. I had even chosen a career in finance which was expected of me, despite having different interests. I realized that I needed to dig deeper to find my own path.

It took years for me to realize that I should be the driving force of my own life and that it is up to me to choose how I want to live and what sort of legacy I am proud to leave behind. The notion that life passes by quickly and not having lived to your fullest potential for years can be extremely tough. I pushed myself out of my comfort zone.

TABLE OF CONTENTS

PREFACE

While writing this book, Coronavirus is spreading throughout Europe and the rest of the world at a fast pace. There is a sense of urgency to life. To set up the right priorities, to spend time with the ones you love, and to contribute to society at large.

Becoming Queen Bee is based on our personal longing for guidance as young girls. A book, we wish we had come across earlier in life, but one which is never too late to read. We are all familiar with the years when we struggle with existential questions and wonder how life is going to turn out. We all long for a recipe for success or at least some answers.

There are no books with all the answers and not one recipe for success. Everyone has their own journey to take. Life will take you on a ride and we want to make sure that you don't only hang on, but that you steer it in the direction you want. We want you to feel proud and satisfied with your chosen direction, with your achievements and your priorities.

The goal with this book is to help you be the best version of yourself with the hand that you're dealt. To leverage your uniqueness without competing or comparing yourself to others. Unlimited by fear, society, and expectations. You have a unique voice and story. A personal purpose waiting to be explored.

Schedule a date night with yourself and let this book guide you and provide you with easy tools to formalize what it is you can and would like to do in your life. Through an easy 3-step transformation process you will get closer to a life of clarity. The book connects people from all corners of the world, shares inspirational stories, and positively encourages everyone to design their purpose-driven life.

"There is no greater agony than bearing an untold story inside you."
- Maya Angelou

THE HUMAN QUEST -
A MEANINGFUL LIFE

It might sound very spiritual to pursue a higher meaning in life, but the fact is that it is one of the most important existential questions we can ask ourselves. Most people carry this question with them throughout life to a certain degree, whether it is consciously or subconsciously. You are certainly not surprised to know that the world's most commonly searched question on Google is *"What is the meaning of life?"*

So, let's start our journey right there, shall we?

Too many people go through life with a sense of emptiness and a lack of purpose. A feeling that every day is the same. You get up, go to work, have dinner, and go to bed again. Just to repeat the next day, interrupted by the occasional "happening". Throughout our own lives, we have often had the thought ourselves, or heard friends say *"I feel like I am wasting my life. Things feel so pointless, and I am already halfway through it"*.

This is in fact normal. It would be strange if you never at some point in life felt depressed or perceived a lack of meaning. It can be that you face a disproportionately high number of problems, that luck is just not on your side, or that you have become a person not in tune with who you really are.

You might be drifting through your own life. A life that has taken you on a ride where you are merely hanging on. You have ended up in a profession you dislike and in a life situation that you would never have chosen. Instead of planning and following your heart, you drift along.

This might be because you are too busy to even reflect. Life passes by and you realize that there is not enough time nor enough energy to do the things you really enjoy. The luxury to explore your true passions don't seem to be in your cards. There is a constant lack of something. It could be financial resources, time, or skills. Or at least that is how it feels.

It all comes down to a lack of a clear personal purpose in life. You lack a game plan.

When you have no meaningful reason for being and can't connect what you are doing to a higher purpose, you are not enjoying and exploring life to the fullest.

The philosopher Aristotle argued that the meaning of life is based on the notion that each person's life has a purpose and that the function of one's life is to attain that purpose. [1]

Imagine waking up every day for your whole life without a purpose. Working with something you dislike or walking around with a nagging feeling that something is missing. The old cliché that *"Life is too short"* is nothing but true. How heartbreaking to all of a sudden realize that you live below your full capacity and not according to your own goals.

Did you know that the most common regret people have on their deathbed is, "I wish I'd had the courage to live a life true to myself, not the life others expected of me". When people realize that their life is almost over, it is easy to see how many dreams have gone unfulfilled.

This makes me think of my own grandmother. One of the first female judges in Sweden who managed to pursue her dream to become a judge despite having six children and going through a divorce. Breaking two taboos of this time, one to divorce and the second to be a woman in a male dominated profession. She challenged the norms and paved the way for us.

Now, let's explore your dreams and plan for a more fulfilled life. One way to do so is to go through our method called the Queen Bee BRAVE Transformation Model™.

Bold Change is the first step to start your transformation of self-exploration. It is important to explore your options freely to define what kind of person you really are, without expectations or boundaries. To explore these options, you might be forced to **Rock Your Comfort Zone**. A change which can be uncomfortable or scary and require a lot of courage.

However, this is fundamental for designing your **Authentic Life** - with a purpose of your own. It will challenge you and it will make you feel **Vulnerable**. But you are not alone, you will learn from others and find inspiration and common ground in their stories. You will read true life brave stories from people who have gone through some kind of transformation themselves.

We will provide tools and concrete methods for empowering you to take control of your life. Life is a journey, and you must go through life's teachings. You will make mistakes and that is ok - you will learn from them. But there is no reason why you should not have a game plan. How to be your best you and **Enjoy** life.

"Knowing yourself is the
beginning of all wisdom."
- Aristotle

BOLD CHANGE

BRAVERY - THE BIG GAME CHANGER

Bravery is the foundation for finding your purpose and to dare following your path. The world is full of opportunities and every corner has something to offer. Through your life journey, you pass by people who seem very capable and able to accomplish extraordinary things in their lives. You might ask yourself why some people follow their purpose and seem to live their dream lives, and some don't. A substantial answer to this is courage.

"Fortune favors the brave."
- Virgil (70 – 19 BCE)

These people have not been afraid to take daring choices. They have simply refused and neglected the feeling of fear. They have continued to follow their passion and kept their focus which has allowed them to develop. They have not given up no matter the circumstances and they have not been afraid of the thought of failure.

Let's take a closer look at what bravery means and how it is possible to find the courage needed to dare to follow your purpose.

Bravery is a difficult word to describe as it has a lot of different meanings to people depending on whom you ask. What we know is that to be brave you need to step out of your comfort zone and to not be afraid to take risks. Basically, it means to push yourself to do things that you wouldn't normally do or to do things that you don't feel comfortable with doing. When we push ourselves, we learn how to grow. The best explanation is that bravery is something that we can practice. All of us can be our best and reach our full potential, even during times when we feel afraid, vulnerable, or anxious.

I have throughout the years heard friends say how bored and tired they are of their jobs or their situations for so many different reasons. Some say that they don't connect with the corporate culture, some have under stimulating tasks and some can't stand their boss or colleagues. Others might just feel unsatisfied and unseen. The most common feeling for all, regardless of the reason, is that they feel like they are wasting their time and they are all ready for a new beginning.

In their mind, they want to change so badly and focus on something that is much more important to them. However, for so many, the years are just passing by and so is their life. All of a sudden, a decade has passed, and they are still within that same shitty job or situation.

The main reason for these limitations is fear. Children are often more fearless than adults. As we grow older, we are shaped to fit into society and to conform. It is easier and less stressful to take the well-trodden path and follow the masses. People don't want to leave their safety net which has taken years to build up and this is often, the only thing known to them. They are familiar with a certain way, with which they feel comfortable. It is the fear of doing something differently, out of the norm.

Another fear is the fear of change. It is scary to be thrown into something which holds uncertainty, where you don't know the outcome, and you lack previous experience. When you haven't tried something before, you obviously don't know how it will turn out.

When you take on something new, you let go of something in the past, sort of like adding rungs to the top of a ladder while the lower ones fade away. And letting go of something in the past can make you feel uncomfortable and scared. You are moving to a place that is unfamiliar to you which requires a different behavior.

"If you do what you've always done,
you'll get what you've always gotten."
- Tony Robbins

As you can see, bravery is needed to deal with change and change is a bit like learning something from scratch, such as learning how to swim. Even though the change is for the better, it is always difficult because it makes you take on new grounds, it brings you to a new territory where you haven't been before.

Change can be a very positive experience, but it is often very emotional, and not always enjoyable. It is something that can give us anxiety because it holds uncertainty and it's unpredictable. Throughout our lives, whether it's personal or professional, we have to embrace change and be open to it, while looking at the different opportunities it holds.

 MARIE FALKENBERG ON CHANGE

Looking at my life, I live for adventure. In Sweden we have an expression that says, "I have ants in my butt," which means that we are not able to sit still, and this phrase really explains me well.

I remember while living in Sweden, I heard a lot about Dubai - how the economy was booming, how you could make tax free money, how the sun was shining, etc. At that time, it was a different and less well-known place than it is today. Dubai caught my attention, and I said to myself that this was the place I would move to, to experience a completely different life.

I arrived in Dubai, 23 years old without friends, no job, and no place to live. Even though I was slightly concerned about how everything was going to turn out, I told myself - if everything goes down the drain and I feel miserable I will just hop on a plane and go back home. With this in my back pocket, everything felt so much easier. I knew that I had to go, I didn't want to visualize myself a few years down the line having said no to a great opportunity due to fear.

Thus, even if the fear is there and we are accepting the challenge of new experiences, gradually the fears will disappear. This will result in an improved self-esteem when we see that we can handle the situation.

INSPIRATION - BRAVERY

 INTERVIEW ANNIE SEEL

A Firestarter Equipped with Fearless
Passion and Finnish Sisu

Someone who truly has lived a life of bravery is Annie Seel. She is not only an enduro racer and rally car driver who rode to Everest base camp on a motorcycle, she is also an expert in dealing with fear and how to run your own race.

Photo by alexochmartin.se

When we called Annie, she was sitting in her kitchen at home in Stockholm, Sweden. She wasn't supposed to be there at this time of the year, however, the pandemic postponed most of her plans. Annie is a Swedish-born motorcyclist with a world altitude record for riding to Mount Everest base camp on a motorcycle. She is also known as an enduro racer and a leading female competitor in the Paris-Dakar Rally.

"I have always been a firestarter," Annie begins when we call her up. Things happen around her.

Already as a young girl, Annie's curiosity got her to question everything, and she felt a need to grasp the bigger picture. Only by understanding the bigger picture, was she able to identify gaps and unexplored areas. This in turn, later in life, helped her identify opportunities for unconventional services or business ideas. It might also have been what led her into doing what no one else had done before; breaking the world altitude record by riding a motorcycle to Mount Everest.

"I have done something, no other person among eight billion people has done."

Annie explains that you don't necessarily have to be best at something, but by doing something differently, you avoid the comparison to others, and it provides you with a unique positioning.

Annie is very versatile, something that becomes evident, both when talking to her but also by looking at the path she has taken in life. In the early years of her career, she worked for IBM and later spent many years setting up a marketing agency. However, she felt a void. A feeling of dissatisfaction led her to ask what she was supposed to achieve in life and if this was it?

"It was the wrong place for me to be, and it slowly killed my creativity and personal identity," she recalls. Annie realized she needed to do her own thing and needed to focus on her passions. She had always loved motorsport and at the age of 35,

she turned this passion into her profession and was soon competing on an elite level.

Her reasoning was simple. *"Why use all that time to benefit others when I can use my drive and passion to build my own career?"* Some people called her egoistic and crazy, but she stood by her decision. Today her achievements within motorsport are ground-breaking and she serves as an inspiration for bravery. This bravery helped her push boundaries in dangerous competitions and challenges, but also to choose her own path.

Annie's approach to bravery is to do and try. Even if you initially fail, you will most likely succeed at the end and you should never underestimate the learnings from failure. *"The bravery needed in motorsport competitions can also be applied to entrepreneurship and to find your courage to follow a passion,"* she says.

> ## *"Of course, there is always a shit factor: shit can always happen, you can just hope it happens to someone else."*
> - Annie laughs.

Annie learned as a young girl that there are alternative ways to achieve what you want. She loved horses and dreamt of having her own horse, but her family did not have the financial means to sustain her passion. *"I started to help out in the stable for free just to be close to the horses",* she recalls.

She also loved dogs but didn't get one, so instead, she arranged a dog jumping competition and managed to get food and prizes sponsored. For her, this helped her realize at a young age that you can start small and work your way towards reaching your dreams. The benefit of starting something sustainable on a grass root level is that you are able to see if it grows organically.

Fear is not an uncommon feeling for Annie. Facing everything from losing control of the bike to facing financial instability. She knows that there will always be doubt or insecurity, but you just have to face failure if and when it happens. If you know what you want, you will put in the hard work needed.

She trusts her Finnish sisu[2] will take her through the current recession. Bravery runs in her veins. Her mother came to Sweden as a Finnish refugee and her grandmother survived two world wars. *"My mother has a strong can-do-it attitude and conviction. She managed to build up a completely new life for us in Sweden,"* Annie says.

Growing up with a single mother, Annie had to help out a lot at home. There was no use complaining as there were no easy escapes. However, despite her young age, she realized that she too could contribute something.

"A small stone is part of a monument."

"You can complain, cry for a while and get angry, but then you have to keep going. You have to try and try again. The important thing is to conquer your own fear. It will be scary, inconvenient, and you will hesitate. You will also have to be prepared to crash maybe one, three, or ten times."

Annie is keen to keep her projects fun. She needs to be interested. Her consultancy "Happy Industries" offers motivational speeches that combine mindset, goal setting, and the useful craziness with hard work and the ability to stand up after you've fallen down. Seel was awarded the Swedish "Adventurer of The Year" award in 2005 and to top it off she is also a serial entrepreneur and a marketing consultant. *"Of course, everything can't be fun all the time but do something which interests you,"* she concludes.

To keep her grounded and to provide support Annie has her rocks of support. One of them is her sister.

Another important insight Annie stresses, is the importance of not clinging too much to materialistic values. By being surrounded by less clutter you are more flexible and have the possibility to shrink the costume if needed. Annie doesn't need luxuries to feel happy and feels she is better off investing in something that creates purpose. A purpose disconnected from money and rather based on self-fulfillment, adventure, and passion.

Today, Annie is considering her next move. The scheduled competitions in Chechnya, Mexico, and California are all canceled. So is her speaker gig at one of the largest motivational conferences in Sweden where she was due to talk under the motto, "No one remembers a coward". The Coronavirus epidemic has forced her to tweak her business model. But thanks to many different revenue streams and flexibility she has been able to do just that.

At the end of the interview when asked about her next move, Annie's voice is full of passion. Her latest potential project is combining her motorcycle skills with a purpose to do good. A project which involves motorcycle ambulances in Tanzania.

"Run your own race."
- Annie Seel

 Annie on Bravery

Annie sees bravery as a muscle that you need to practice. That something becomes less scary once you have practiced it a couple of times. By daring to challenge yourself with different projects you are more resistant to failures. You know that you have survived before, and the comfort of knowing that reassures you that it will most likely work this time as well.

 Annie on Fear

To cope with fear Annie likes to apply risk management. The same method as when preparing for a race. By making sure her motorcycle is in the best condition, her health is on top and she is well prepared for the competition, she minimizes potential risks.

Benefits of Diversity

Annie stresses the importance of doing and trying. That the big goal could be broken into small achievements. You might not have to leave your corporate job, but you can pursue your passions outside of your day job. By exploring projects on the side and by being flexible you are diversifying your risks.

Learn more about Annie Seel, Happy Industries and Only Women Drivers Club by connecting @ LinkedIn/AnnieSeel

Stockholm Rally School: www.stockholmrallyschool.com

BEING FEARLESS

For an adventurer like Annie, she is used to facing fear. Most of us will face fear in different forms and it is difficult when it hits us. But fear is just a feeling, a signal, and it should not make us run away. Regardless, if the challenge contains difficulties or opportunities. We should rather embrace it and challenge it. Remember, that the feeling of fear can indicate that something exciting is about to happen and can be the start of a new fantastic beginning.

Establishing fearlessness can range from smaller things such as having a daring conversation with somebody to a more adventurous activity, like starting your own company. It could also be a dream that you have wanted to achieve for a very long time.

"He who has overcome his fears will truly be free."
- Aristotle

Remember, you are not the only one to feel fear - we all do. You need to learn how to deal with it and the first thing you can do is acknowledge that you have fears and accept that they exist. Only after acceptance are you able to understand fear better.

Let's look at some of the ways to handle fear.

One of them is to embrace failure. You need to allow yourself to fail. When we think of failure, we tend to tell ourselves that it is not an option and most of us are good at repeating that sentence, however, we should rather say that failure is an option. So, what if something didn't work out? It is not the end of the world. At least you tried. Maybe it will work better on your next attempt. And remember, you don't always have to be perfect at every single little thing.

When I wanted to switch careers after close to 20 years in the banking industry, I was really worried. I constantly kept on thinking about the worst-case scenario. What could happen to me if I just quit? Would my successful career be over? Would I be employable in another industry? Could I come back to my job if I changed my mind?

At the same time, I kept telling myself what the cost would be to try something new? And how likely is it that the things I fear will actually happen? By doing this, I realized that the worse-case scenario was actually not that bad and that I had more to gain rather than to lose. – Marie Falkenberg

The good news is fearlessness is something that you can practice. It can inspire you rather than defeat you. Practice it daily until it becomes a routine. Life is a constant fight against our comfort zone - you push it, and it pushes you back.

When you push yourself, you learn how to grow. Bravery tends to unfold one situation at a time, experience after experience, as we go along. A courageous act doesn't have to be an extreme sport. Every single day of our lives there is an opportunity to be brave.

It could be something simple like having a conversation with somebody about something that you kept inside for a while, or it could be saying yes to an opportunity.

Fear tends to be the prime reason for holding us back, which is interesting since we live in a fast-moving world where change needs to be endorsed. The biggest threat to any individual or organization's growth and goals is when people fear calculated risk-taking.

From my corporate experience, I have seen how fear can limit people, especially when they have to make decisions and take risks. As calculated as the risks might be, they tend to always ask for a second and third opinion before they dare to execute. People are not used to acting brave, they rather wait and do what they are being told.

We need to start speaking more about what it means to be brave and how we can overcome the fear so that it does not stop us from taking action. Courageous people do feel fear, but they are better equipped to manage and overcome it.

What is the worst that can happen to us if we stop taking risks?

Well, nothing extraordinary in your life might happen to you but your personal goals, ambitions, visions, and dreams might not come through. What is important to keep in mind at all times is that life is a risk in itself. This is something basic that takes understanding. We need to remember that if we don't necessarily take any risks and only play it safe, we risk everything.

" Courage is not the absence of fear,
but the triumph over it. "
- Nelson Mandela

 MARIE FALKENBERG

I had everything in life, or so I thought. An unexpected wake-up call changed my direction.

I believe many of us carefully listen to our parents as we grow up and we tend to follow their advice for what they believe is the best way forward for our lives. This is what I did.

Everything was going smoothly – I lived a fun expat life, and I was a vice president with a great salary working in a tax haven. Everything was going steady. One morning when reaching the office, I had received a calendar invite about a meeting with the president of the division, it was nothing very unusual. The calendar invite just said: "Catch-up meeting" and it was supposed to be held in one of our conference rooms further down the corridor.

The meeting turned out to be shorter than what I expected. He said, "I can see that your passion for your work is gone, I am not sure what has happened to you? Are you sure you really want this?"

I took a deep breath and said, "I don't know; in fact, I feel confused."

I recall how his words just sucked the breath out of me and before I left that conference room I said, "You are right, I lack passion."

I left the conference room and drove back home. As I got home, I crawled into bed and hid underneath the blanket crying for a few hours, while stuffing myself with chocolate.

I can continue telling you in further detail about how I felt and what it did to my self-esteem and my finances etc. but - I now realize that conversation created one of the strongest discomforts I had ever felt. It was that discomfort, the departure of my organized life, that forever changed it for the better. In the end, what makes us comfortable can really ruin us, and what makes us uncomfortable is the only way we can continue to grow.

If somebody had told me on that day when I received that calendar invite: "Marie, your boss having that conversation with you, saying that you lacked passion, is a good thing for you because now you can really think of what you want to do. It will help you grow. You should really be thankful!"

At that moment, I would have felt so frustrated to hear those words.

However, I quickly became motivated to start a new chapter of my life. I went back to school to do an MBA and I took help from mentors to transform my life.

 DARE TO DREAM

Dare to imagine yourself a few years from today. What accomplishments would you have wanted to achieve? What sort of impact would you have loved to make? What kind of legacy would you want to leave and how would you want to make a difference? Stop here for a bit and think about what is important for you.

EXAMPLES

- Create a legacy
- Make a difference
- Follow your dreams more
- Make an impact in the world
- Practice kindness
- Be close to people you love / who make you feel good
- Become a leader in your profession
- Inspire others / be a role model
- Live in the present

Remember to think big. Write what comes to mind. Remember these dreams will most likely change. This exercise will help you define what is of importance to you.

1.	
2.	
3.	
4.	
5.	
6.	
7.	
8.	
9.	
10.	

 Remember you can practice bravery like a muscle. Think about what bravery means for you and challenge yourself to one brave action a week.

ROCK YOUR COMFORT ZONE

We have explored Chapter one and the letter **B,** and the concept of "Bold Change". We have discussed how you can practice bravery as a muscle to get used to it, and how you can make challenges less scary. We have explored how easy it is to continue a comfortable life, but we have identified what you can gain from being fearless. Bravery is an important tool when you embark on the journey to a life of purpose.

Let's continue with **R** which is to **"Rock your Comfort Zone"**. Stepping out of one's comfort zone enables you to dare to follow your passions and personal purpose. To leave the comfort zone can mean a lot of different things such as leaving a job, pursuing a dream, leaving a certain role that you are familiar with, leaving a relationship, or standing up for yourself.

To step out of your comfort zone might be essential to follow your purpose but it might also not be. However, to give yourself a fuller life, you have to dare to think out of the box and freely explore beyond the limitations of comfort.

As human beings, we are inclined to live like guppies in relation to others. It is important for us to feel a sense of belonging, and the herd to which we belong affects our behavior. Doing what everyone else is doing gives us a feeling of comfort. This is not necessarily a bad thing as we gain strength and comfort from others and for some, this in itself is the purpose of life. However, this can limit you since you are not inclined to think outside the box or do something outside of common behavior. We might measure our achievements through the eyes of others more than our own, and that is not living with authenticity to oneself.

For the one brave enough to choose their own path, the reward could be a feeling of self-fulfillment and a true exploration of personal purpose. It is important to understand how this phenomenon most likely has influenced you. By realization, it will be easier to take action to live more in line with your true self.

The struggle which goes on within the comfort zone is often referred to as the rat race. The term rat race is described as *"A way of life in which people are caught up in a fiercely competitive struggle for wealth or power".* The rat race often traps you in a safe and publicly approved route without you even noticing. People often end up in two parallel rat races: one driven by peers and the other one dictated by society.

"Normal is getting dressed in clothes that you buy for work, driving through traffic in a car that you are still paying for, in order to get to a job that you need so you can pay for the clothes, car and the house that you leave empty all day in order to afford to live in it."
- Ellen Goodman

PEER PRESSURE

You might have thought peer pressure belonged only to your teenage years but that is not true. It just enters your life in a more subtle and less obvious way when you are older. Peer pressure can take many forms. You might have this friend who is always making you feel guilty and not enough. You might feel pressured to find a partner and start a family because this is what everyone else does.

Common peer pressure dictates that you have to achieve a certain status. This status depends on the clique of people you identify with and the people you surround yourself with. If you are an artist, the pressure might be that you should live in poverty, work long hours in a studio, and live in a low-income, up and coming area of town. While this may be a stereotype, you get the point.

On the other hand, this is just as limiting as being a banker, feeling the pressure to settle in an affluent area, ensuring you leave work after your boss, and being lonely due to a lack of social time.

There is good and there is bad peer pressure. Sometimes this kind of pressure can help push you out of your comfort zone and you will feel influenced to be better. However, negative peer pressure leads you to behave in ways that contradict your true values. Contradicting your true values can hurt your self-esteem and take you further away from your personal purpose.

A recent study published in the journal *Developmental Psychology*[3] found that resistance to peer pressure increases dramatically between the ages of 14 and 18 years old but remains virtually unchanged between the ages of 18 and 30 years old. Middle adolescence is an especially significant period for the development of the capacity to stand up for what one believes and resist the pressures of one's peers to do otherwise.

It is an interesting thought that you are actually more aware and better equipped to handle peer pressure earlier in life. This would incline that you regard peer pressure as something which belongs in the past and that it doesn't affect you as much as an adult, when it actually does.

Whatever is your "golden cage", there are ways to deal with peer pressure. The first step is to identify how, and which peer pressure affects you. It is important to identify the expectations and pressure you feel from your peers in order for you to be able to disregard it and live on your own terms. The race is a mindset. You can be a millionaire but still, be stuck in the race.

Another solution to try avoid peer pressure is to widen your circle and develop relationships across your usual clique of friends. This is also a splendid opportunity to improve your network and to challenge yourself to create friendships outside your comfort zone.

Remember yourself and your values. When you have defined your personal purpose and your action plan, it will be much easier to stay on course and true to yourself.

SOCIETAL PRESSURE

Societal pressure makes us compete in another kind of race. From birth, we are placed in social structures. We are put in school and taught to listen and follow. This is something that will also help prepare us for a corporate structure of following the leader and compliance.

Then we are taught that a certain school might be the only way to lead us to a certain career. For example, you don't become a McKinsey consultant if you haven't been to Stanford. You can't become an academic author if you haven't studied at Oxford, and the list goes on.

"Be yourself everyone else is already taken."
- Oscar Wilde

This kind of pressure can kill many dreams before they are even embarked upon.

Now you might be nodding to yourself, *"Yes, but that is how it is."* If so, then you haven't considered how society has changed. We will go through some of the benefits of society today in a little while, but with curiosity and determination you can achieve a lot when it comes to attaining skills and getting closer to your dreams. Most kids today explore passions and are self-taught online from an early age. More people than ever are making money from their passions. An independent mindset and a creative skillset are the tools for the future and will be an essential skill when robots and automation handle the more mundane tasks of the working force.

Besides the educational stereotypes, there are many examples of societal pressure in life. Pressures which may or may not hinder us from following our authenticity. The concept of marriage, religion, and lifestyle are other examples. As with peer pressure, it is essential that you identify which of these societal pressures affects you.

Also, be aware of and make sure that you are able to identify the "what is to be expected" traps. The things you are expected to do in life, and which are so easy to just do. Be alert and make sure these expectations are actually in line with your values and tap into what you are trying to achieve. It might be that all your friends are moving to a certain area of town but when you come to think about it, you prefer another area. It might be that it is expected that you study medicine because everyone in your family did so before you, but for you it sounds boring.

You should also be aware of the "perfect people" who surround you on social media. Know that much of this is a facade and the happiest lives are lived away from your mobile phone while you are comparing yourself to your own goals.

Much of this pressure is pressure that you allow to happen.

As with any pressure, a clear personal purpose and action plan will keep you on your authentic path. Ask yourself why you are doing a certain thing. Let it go through your authenticity filter to make sure the decision is made in line with your values, hopes and dreams.

As with bravery, you can practice breaking the social norms. It will be easier every time and it will help you understand where the boundaries are and that it isn't going to hurt you to step beyond those boundaries. It will become less scary every time, and you will realize it added something to your life.

It is not an easy task to break free from expectations, whether they come from peers or society. Belonging to a certain group gives us comfort and it can help our careers take off. We might be doing it without even reflecting upon it. However, make sure everything you do is in line with you.

 # LIST YOUR PRESSURES AND ROADBLOCKS

Ghosts disappear when you turn on the lights in the closet. There are many pressures and roadblocks that hinder your personal development, but once you illuminate them, they become less influential and scary. Below are examples of some feelings which can come with breaking out of the norm.

FEARS SURROUNDING BREAKING FREE FROM PEER AND SOCIETAL PRESSURE

- Feeling isolated or lonely

- Losing some of your identity and status

- Everyone thinks you are insane

FEARS OF CHANGING YOUR STRUCTURE AND CURRENT PATH

- Stepping into the unknown

- What about savings, high expenses: a heavy mortgage/rent, bills, children, liabilities

- Being perceived as less valuable to the business

- Loss of career and getting passed over for promotions

COMMON MENTAL ROADBLOCKS

- It's kind of good as it is

- I am worried that a flexible lifestyle will turn me into a hot mess due to a lack of structure and routine

- I don't have the time

- It has all been done before

- I don't have the skill set or the education

List the fears and roadblocks which hold you back. By clearly visualizing the worst-case scenarios you are able to see that they probably aren't as bad as you have made them in your head. Often the what-ifs are manageable and can be turned into positives. We will go through this more in-depth as we go along.

Fears / Roadblocks
1.
2.
3.
4.
5.
6.
7.
8.
9.

 As with bravery you can practice stepping out of your comfort zone. Do something unexpected and out of the ordinary to practice how it feels. While doing it, you will realize that it wasn't as bad as you thought, and you will be more prone to take the leap.

INSPIRATION TO ROCK
YOUR COMFORT ZONE

 INTERVIEW ILJA STENBERG

Ilja Stenberg Moved from Stockholm
to Tbilisi and Opened a Boutique Hotel

Without any hotel experience, Ilja fell in love with Tbilisi, the capital of the country Georgia, and decided to settle there and open a small hotel. The hotel has only six rooms, but she has now opened a cafè bar and food delivery business. Her venture has received top reviews in well-known international travel guides.

Photo by Maurice Wolf

Ilja took the step to make a dramatic change from her current set-up when she left her conventional life to try something new somewhere else. By selling her apartment she managed to buy a small hotel in a country far away. Her journey has been a challenge but also an achievement which has brought her closer to her purpose to challenge herself and learn new things. Follow her journey on how she took the leap…

When Ilja was in her early 30s she lived in her hometown of Stockholm and worked in a cult cinema for independent movies, specializing in distribution, events, and outreach for Nordic and international documentaries.

Her work had taken a toll on her and she felt overworked and exhausted. She knew that she wanted to do something different. She had an urge to leave the country for quite some time but was unsure of where to go and what to do. She was waiting for that brilliant opportunity to come along. Or maybe a friend who wanted to join her.

I am sure you can relate to the behavior of waiting for the knock on your door or the phone call to change your life.

At some point, she decided it was useless to wait for the right opportunity. She had been to Tbilisi, Georgia before and loved the place. There was magic in this city and something about the unexpected, unpredictable atmosphere of the country resonated with her.

"It is something like a Haruki Murakami book, I would not be surprised to see two moons in the sky in Georgia!"

The country is upside-down. It is filled with culture, dance, food, singing, and nature. She took a job arranging a film festival in Georgia together with the Swedish Institute. It was not well paid, but it gave her some time to breathe. Her plan was to travel afterward, while figuring out her next step.

Sometimes destiny steps in. Ilja came across a small boutique hotel for sale by a Georgian couple. They had two hotels in the city but had recently moved to London and therefore decided to sell one. It was a small boutique hotel with only six rooms, but the interior was exquisite, and she was intrigued by its discreet charm.

Ilja sold her apartment in the quite overpriced Stockholm town, and with the help of friends she borrowed money for the down payment.

"I had fantastic friends who helped me."

Her friends had recently sold their own apartments, so they had cash, and she promised to pay them back as soon as her own apartment was sold.

In September 2017, she opened the doors to Ilja's Hotel on a quiet residential street in the inner city of Tbilisi. It is located in a bohemian part of town with old brick buildings and wrought-iron balconies, like in 1920's Paris. The hotel was to serve as an oasis that would provide guests with a safe haven in the otherwise chaotic city.

The journey was not easy. With no knowledge of the local language and no previous hotel experience, she had to find people to trust. She remembers carrying the money for the hotel in cash and handing it over to a public notary without the reassurance that the property was actually hers. In Georgia, these things take time and work a bit differently, to say the least. In the middle of the process, she was also traveling to Berlin, and somewhere there the stress took its toll on her. She remembers fainting on the airplane, waking up next to a concerned stewardess helping her to oxygen. The process turned out to be nothing for the faint-hearted.

When asked why she decided to take this plunge, she explained, *"I felt that I was really bad at finishing things. When I went to dance class instead of doing my exam to advance to the next level, I preferred doing the beginner's class again. I didn't want to avoid hurdles."*

"The hotel would help my personal development. An achievement. Something in my name."

When she called her mother in distress over the fact that she had bought a hotel, she received the comforting words that it was indeed just a small hostel. *"That is very much my mum,"* she said laughing. *"My mother has always been very adventurous herself and that has probably made it easier for me to take the leap"*, she concluded.

Today she has opened a small café and transformed the lower level into an apartment for herself. The hotel is going as good as it can, with its limited number of rooms, but then Coronavirus hit. For now, the hotel is closed, and she has transformed the café business into a delivery service through the Georgian equivalent of Uber Eats. Thankfully, salaries are quite low in Georgia, and she hopes her business manages to sustain through the imposed quarantine.

Altogether she looks back at the journey, *"It has been very rewarding and fun to meet all fantastic guests,"* she concludes. *"Some I have even developed a friendship with. It is in general very interesting people coming to Georgia as it is still quite an unconventional destination."*

Ilja was told that it was essential to keep consistency in the hotel offerings and routines, but that proved to be very difficult in an inconsistent country as Georgia. Often specific ingredients run out and you have to reinvent and be creative.

What she finds liberating in Georgia is that due to economical desperation and fewer rules, people open up businesses every day. Some might not be open for a long time, but they try, and they are not afraid to fail. *"One purpose in life I have had is to learn and this has certainly been a valuable learning experience,"* Ilja concludes.

"Who knows I might be doing something else one day,
but I am grateful for this experience."

Photo by Guram Muradov

For more information, check out Ilja's Hotel: www.iljashotel.com

THE PLAYING FIELD /
SOCIETY OF TODAY

It becomes less scary to leave your comfort zone if you consider the society we live in today. It has probably never been as fast-changing and as easy to explore new passions with less risk as it is today. Let's take a quick look at the current playing field and how you can benefit from when it comes to exploring your passions.

In the late 1700s, the industrial revolution brought us technology, which in turn increased productivity and mass production. Suddenly livelihoods based on agriculture and handicrafts transformed into large-scale industry and manufacturing. Many people had to be flexible and change professions.

This important milestone impacted our current society, and this development has not ceased. It is estimated that 800 million people globally could be made redundant by technology over the next ten years according to a recent study by the McKinsey Global Institute. Depending on when you read this book, we might not be quite there yet, but it is fair to assume that self-driving vehicles based on AI will impact the profession of truck drivers. Cashiers are already being replaced by automatic tills and bicycle couriers might soon be made redundant with drones. There is a constant evolution and technology has been an integral part of the change we have seen in life since the industrial revolution took off.

"It's easier to change what you do than people think it is. If you don't change, your field changes around you."
- Walter Gilbert

Our lives are constantly impacted by a steady stream of revolutionary inventions and comfortable personal gadgets. This has been going on since the invention of the steam engine to the first computers and most recently AI and machine learning. Consider how mobile devices have impacted our professional lives by keeping us always connected and always on.

Robotics and automation are about to change society in a major way. Many people, often those in more traditional professions, are afraid of the implications of this change and do their best to resist it. If your professional career or livelihood is in jeopardy, this is of course a rational response.

For our personal journeys we need to be prepared, seize opportunities, and be able to adapt to these changes. There are several advantages coming with the wave of change. Especially when it comes to the flexibility and freedom it provides us to explore purpose. Let's look at some of these benefits.

MAKE IT WORK FOR YOU

An interesting advantage today is how easy it is to explore new careers and develop new skills. The rise of technology has completely transformed our possibilities for learning. This change comes in the form of MOOCs and the ability to learn on the web. There is nothing that you can't find a tutorial for online.

A massive open online course (MOOC /muːk/) is an online course aimed at unlimited participation and open access via the web.

- Wikipedia

MOOCs future potential impact on the educational system is enormous. We haven't seen the transformation on a large scale yet due to several reasons. One important reason is the impact of societal pressure: the notion that you should enroll and be physically present at a campus. Another reason is that the technology is not quite there yet. The lack of live instruction with interaction in these courses makes them less engaging. Although many students sign up for a course, very few actually finish them.

But there is a major shift slowly taking place. It is fair to assume that this transformation will take some time yet, but it will have a major impact on the entire school system once it does. Just imagine the economic implications for such a change. Since 2000 there has been an increase in tuition cost by 72 percent, whereas earnings for people aged 25-30 years old have decreased by 15 percent[4]. The current set-up is not sustainable.

Free online courses can be a powerful tool to cope with the ongoing transformation in industries, but they can also encourage flexibility in acquiring new skills and exploring passions. Today top universities such as Harvard, Yale, and MIT provide free online courses for the eager. They provide an affordable and flexible way to learn new skills and advance one's career without the limitation of funds or locality.

So, consider this a strength and an excellent tool to acquire a new skill set and to explore passions.

Another potential benefit society today brings us when it comes to pursuing our passions is the Gig Economy. The defining moment of the rise of the Gig Economy took off after the Great Recession in the US during 2008 when people were forced to find alternative ways to support themselves. Collapsing housing markets and rising unemployment rates led people to take whatever jobs they could get, despite them being temporary.

With the Gig Economy the labor market can hire temporary, contracted workers instead of traditional employees. It sadly entails insecurity around job security or benefits but with more advanced technology applications, this economy is booming.

A study by the McKinsey Global Institute estimated that up to 162 million people in the United States and Europe - or 20 to 30 percent of the working-age population - are engaged in some kind of independent work.

It is also predicted that if the gig economy keeps growing at its current rate, more than 50% of the US workforce will participate in it by 2027.

Despite its potential flaws, as with everything, there is also an upside. With the Gig Economy, it has never been easier to be flexible.

The rise of online and app-based services such as Uber, Airbnb and Task Rabbit have contributed to gig work's popularity. These services allow you to jump from job to job exploring your passions or can provide you with an income while doing so. You might drive Uber in the evening to support yourself while writing your book, exploring how it is to offer your skills on a freelancer platform while keeping your corporate job, or renting out your house while trying out living in another country.

If you decide to become a small business owner, you are able to try your idea without risking too much since you are able to hire contractors on a job-to-job basis. You are also able to hire temporary teams for projects based on the current needs of your business.

Regardless of what you decide to do you have many possibilities to be more flexible and explore. Use the current possibilities in the market as tools for your journey. Benefit from what is out there.

 LIST WHAT COULD BENEFIT YOU

Think about what could benefit you from the tools we have in society today. An online course you would like to take? A secondary revenue stream which could help you pursue a dream? Or maybe renting out your second home?

1.	
2.	
3.	
4.	
5.	

INSPIRATION - ACQUIRE A NEW SKILL

INTERVIEW NINA HOWDEN

Vision, Hard Work and Determination Led to a Change in Careers and to the Welsh Countryside

Nina and Joe moved from Berlin to Wales and opened Silver Circle Distillery without previous knowledge of the distillation industry. Nina shares their story which changed their location, lifestyles, and careers.

We are contacting Nina while she in the Wye Valley Area of Natural Beauty, a protected landscape at the border between England and Wales. An area famous for its dramatic and scenic rolling hills.

During the summer of 2018, Nina, together with Joe and their two children left Berlin for Wales to start up a gin distillery. In 2019, they had already finished production and in March 2020, they were about to open up their gin experience center for the public. Then the Coronavirus pandemic hit. Now they are surprised by how many consumers find their way to their online store. During the Covid pandemic, they now produce hand sanitizer products, and they are able to refine their experience center.

Their story is very interesting and serves as an inspiration for how passion and determination can enable you to switch professions without previous knowledge. Nina has challenged herself in the past. Her career started in a structured corporation where she specialized in human resources. However, she felt she wanted to do her own thing and moved to Berlin, where she took up the chance to set up her own business.

Since she loved music, she arranged small concerts, and suddenly her network of artists needed public relations services, which in turn started to generate a stable income.

"Sometimes you don't need to have this great vision, you can start small by doing what you like and that, in turn, will grow organically." Nina concludes.

"You just have to start doing something."

To find the courage needed to start something different, you can do the transition one step at a time. *"If your dream is to start a restaurant, why not create pop-up dinners for friends where you charge for food and get people together for an experience?"* Nina asks. *"Sometimes it's better to think less about business. Think about the essence in what you want to do. Which in this case is to cook and provide an enjoyable atmosphere."*

Nina, who is Swedish, and Joe, a Brit, met in a co-working office in Berlin. They both ran their own businesses within the music industry, working with artists and social media.

Two kids later they followed their common dream to move to the English countryside and set up a small distillery. They were both very into cocktails and spirits and loved experimenting with their own infusions. Now they had to learn as much as they could.

"We knew nothing in the beginning, but interest and dedication takes you a long way."

With the help of online learning tools such as YouTube videos, podcasts, and books, they were able to obtain much insight and knowledge. *"Most knowledge within different industries can be obtained online,"* Nina says. After an additional "Fundamentals of Distilling Certificate" in London they both had the technical knowledge to advance.

Photo by Johnny Hathaway

Their distillery in Wales is a passion project with the idea to take the tastes and smells of the valley and bottle it. Their passion for food, drinks, and craftsmanship has led the way and they have set up a welcoming experience center where you get to distill your own gin and gain insight into the production process through tours and tastings.

Their signature product "Wye Valley Gin" has led them to expand their range and develop a series of limited-run seasonal gins, liqueurs, and vodka. Their concept is based on the idea to highlight local flavors and products, and to have a big focus on sustainability.

Most people would find it amazing that they have achieved all this in such a short time but compared to previous start-ups, Nina found the journey long. It is a very complex industry that is highly regulated which requires permits, licenses and advanced equipment. *"It has been essential to break down our main goal into minor targets not to lose focus,"* Nina says.

The adventure has also brought surprising benefits. The couple's craftsmanship has rubbed off on their children and Nina has reconsidered what is important in life. *"The other day my son asked if he could pick some elderflower to make his own lemonade. The children see that we are creating things and it makes them curious. They are able to see that it is possible to create things yourself which tells them that they can too."*

Nina's motivation is not money, but time. To spend time wisely. Materialistic possessions have never been of interest, but rather her own time and achievements. She feels privileged and humbled by the fact that she has the freedom to control her own time and work with what interests her and for herself. In this phase of life, she values being productive, being in a social environment, and controlling her time. *"It feels natural that my life is not divided between job and pleasure,"* she says.

"Despite the hard work, my life is filled with purpose. It feels very meaningful."

Online learning, interest, and determination were the tools necessary for Nina and Joe to dare to set up their distillery. By focusing on the smaller tasks, they have now achieved their larger dream.

Nina's Advice to her Children

In our twenties, we were already focused on making money. For my children, I will tell them otherwise. They should focus on what they enjoy doing. It is ok to live on noodles and drive Uber as long as they explore what they enjoy. When thinking back to your twenties, your fondest memory will not be how steady your income was.

 ## Nina's Advice for the Eager

When embarking on a project like this do the calculations and make sure you have the business plan and a sustainable model. If you know exactly how many bottles you have to sell for the business to survive, and you know it is manageable, it will help you dare to take the step because you are prepared.

Don't forget to visit Nina and Joe if ever in Wales and check out their work at Silver Circle Distillery: www.silvercircledistillery.com

COMBINE CAREER WITH PURPOSE

You may find that your career choice does not connect to your personal purpose. This is a highly individual issue, and it is neither wrong nor right. It might be that you realize that your career choice plays a substantial part in your purpose and something that you have to change. It might also be that your personal purpose will only reflect outside of the confines of your career. Considering how much time you spend on your career, it is of course fantastic if you are doing something that is actually your passion. But this is not the case for many. Make sure your career either aligns with your purpose or enables you to pursue it on the side.

It is surprising how little counseling and help students take advantage of when choosing a career path and studies. Often a career path is based on the ability to make money, skills, expectations, and surprisingly often happenstance.

Recent career advice has been to turn your passion into your career, that it makes you more successful to do something that you enjoy. However, this might or might not be true. That is all good and fantastic if you can combine passion and career, but remember it might not be reasonable to turn your passion into your professional career.

- Your passion might change

- You would not enjoy it in the long run

- It might be impossible for your passion to provide you with financial stability or is not possible for a career

There are other ways to let your career enhance your personal purpose. For example, your personal purpose might contain a level of freedom, and therefore you might pursue a flexible career, that allows flexibility in either working hours or location, to be able to do that.

The consensus is that some people might have their purpose in their career, but this is not true for everyone, and it is also not necessary. However, your career should enhance your level of fulfillment. It should help you feel achieved, tap into your skills, and help you follow your path in life.

 Consider that the average person will change careers five to seven times during their working life. Therefore, acquiring new skills and exploring alternative passions might lead to a different profession either by choice, self-exploration, or can serve as a backup if and when society changes.

 Steve Jobs was a big fan of the "10,000 hours to mastery". A rule based on the study that excellence is not just based on practice but deliberate practice. This is the notion that if you spend 10,000 hours on something, you will be really good at it. This could be done by either improving the skills you already have, extending the reach and range of those skills, or acquiring new ones. Through practice, observation, refinement, and more practice, you are able to master something.

INSPIRATION, PURPOSE & PASSION COMBINED

 INTERVIEW SARAH BELAL

A Troublemaker with a Heart and Passion for Justice

Sarah Belal, Executive Director and Founder of Justice Project Pakistan, found her calling in defending inmates on Pakistan's death row. Sarah integrates her greater purpose directly into her work. For some, this is a must, but it often comes with a major commitment.

Photo by Ali Haider

When we call up Sarah in Lahore, Pakistan, she is worrying about the Coronavirus entering the prison system. Her two daughters are placed in front of an iPad to buy her some time to talk to us. We are excited to learn more about Sarah's story since she has truly lived her passion. She has been fortunate enough to be able to combine her passion with her career which gives her a very strong personal purpose.

Sarah is a US-born Pakistani who spent her early years in American and European schools. Her story to find her calling is a fascinating journey, closely linked to her past.

In Pakistan, her father is, as she describes him, a "successful capitalist", a businessman with factories in the textile industry. Her mother is her biggest supporter and someone who always believes in justice. Both her brothers are entrepreneurs who have based their businesses around co-ownership and giving back to society.

Sarah herself has always been very interested in the question of fairness. *"My mum was complaining that I always nagged 'This is not fair mum'."* The quest for fairness might have been what led her to Oxford for a degree in law. Law in itself was not as interesting as the prospect that it would enable her to engage in human rights.

"My mother is not surprised, I have been arguing since the day I was born."

During an afternoon in Oxford, she found herself listening to a lecture which would prove to have a large impact on what she is doing today. A pro-bono lawyer, together with the mother of a young man they had just saved from death row in the US, emphasized the need to abolish the death penalty. She recalls it being the best spent afternoon during her studies, unaware that it would be an important piece of the puzzle for her own journey.

After her studies, as a newlywed, she decided to move back to Pakistan to live with her husband. Originally, she had no plan to return to Pakistan, which turned out to be a very different country from what she had left behind in the early 90s. Back in Pakistan, her father wanted her to join his business and she decided to give it a go. *"My father convinced me, I could make a difference there, but when I started labor trade unions, he got into trouble,"* she says. *"He soon received angry calls from textile factory owners in the area."*

"Capitalism as a system that demands that you exploit workers,"
- Sarah concludes.

Sarah went back to practicing law but felt depressed. She felt that something was missing and constantly questioned herself and the lack of creating an impact. Her life was convenient, but the nagging feeling in her stomach wouldn't go away. *"I started to feel neurotic about what my place in the world was. I had been waiting for a revelation my whole life."*

While she was depressed and between jobs, her family had enough and staged an intervention. They told her that they didn't care if she liked what she did or if she found meaning in it. The fact that they had spent a lot of money on her education meant that she had to get up and get a job.

Her husband was put in charge of kicking her out of bed at 7 a.m. and she had the option to either work out or look for a job. *"Obviously I decided to have coffee and look for a job,"* Sarah admitted.

"There was no option for me to stay at home and be a bad housewife."

While she was flipping through the editorial pages, she stumbled across a letter from a prisoner on death row. He had one week left to live and had written to the newspaper telling his story and asking for help. He had two small girls and his wife had died while he was in prison. *"The Oxford death row story came to my mind,"* Sarah recalls. She ended up calling the newspaper, not because she wanted to take the case, but she couldn't get his words out of her head and she wanted to at least make sure that some lawyer had called.

"I know what I knew, and it bothered me."

She called the newspaper and after 30 minutes the defendant's brother called her. Within an hour he was at her door with the case files. Sarah, who had never done a death penalty case before, and who had only been out of law school for a year and a half, felt panic.

"I will find you the most competent lawyer because I know a lot of really big lawyers who would do anything to get me out of their office," she told him. *"I will never forget the look on his brother's face because he just looked at me and said, 'No one is going to take this case'."*

He was right. Sarah was told that there was nothing more that could be done, that all appeals had been rejected all up to the supreme court, and his mercy petition was pending.

She was advised to not take the case, that there was nothing more she could do as a lawyer, and that it would be stupid to start her career with an unwinnable case. It would harm her professional reputation.

"First of all, what professional reputation? And secondly, how could you as a lawyer possess a set of skills and not use them. It really is like being a superhero right, you have a set of skills, there are good superheroes, average superheroes, and excellent superheroes. Regardless, you do have a set of skills. How could you not try to use them, even if you fail to help someone who is going to die? What could mean more than just even trying, right?"

Later that night the inmate called her from prison. This was in 2009 and it became the start of her non-profit "Justice Project Pakistan" (JPP). JPP's purpose is to represent the most vulnerable prisoners facing the harshest punishments - providing free legal representation to prisoners on death row and those unlawfully detained in secret prisons around the world.

Sarah will never forget when she visited a prison for the first time. The sun was strong, and she could not avoid the tears as she gazed over at the hanging execution area. The hair on her arms were standing up. There was a silence there you could hear. She could have walked out but she knew she couldn't live with herself if she did. This was what she was meant to do.

What she didn't know then, is that ten years later, JPP lawyers and investigators are still visiting clients every Thursday.

A lawyer on the prison grounds was an unusual sight and soon other prisoners started calling for help. Without much prior experience, Sarah borrowed money, found an office, and managed to put a small team together. A team dedicated enough to take a job with a minimum salary. Her father donated a laptop and with small means, they managed to move the office out of their guestroom.

> ## "It seems like as soon as a new roadblock occurred, we just barely managed to find a solution."

JPP's approach is very hands-on, gathering evidence, and going into the field. Sarah wanted to meet the people she was defending. *"Lawyers don't turn up to prison. That is bad practice and the equivalent of being ambulance chasers in the United States. We don't do that."*

JPP's work was unconventional, being everywhere they needed to be. When TV debates were banned, they were on social media. Alternative communication went through digital space and arts. They collaborated with artists to highlight issues through drama and exhibitions. All outside of what a lawyer is expected to do. *"The profession has changed, and our arena is larger,"* Sarah resonates.

> ## "I am more than just a lawyer in court, and it is rewarding, frustrating, and overwhelming."

When Sarah first arrived in the prison, she could have just walked away. It wouldn't have been on her to fix it. She could have run out of there. She didn't owe anyone anything and there were so many condemned prisoners. But Sarah would never have been able to live with herself if she did and ten years later, she is still visiting clients on Thursdays.

"When you are fighting for someone's life it has to be more than a client-lawyer relationship. My seniors used to say to me 'don't get emotionally invested in the case'. I fundamentally disagree with that. I fight harder and better when I am emotionally invested in a case."

"I think it makes us better at what we do when we have skin in the game and when the stakes are high."

When Pakistan abolishes the death penalty, Sarah will feel satisfied. She believes it will happen, maybe not in five years, but if they are doing what they are doing and keep doing it well, she is sure it will happen.

"And it means something, it means something for the law and for actual people and it means something more for me."

JPP came into being because two women were told that this isn't what a lawyer does and that they must do things a certain way if they were to be taken seriously as lawyers.

Sarah and the team were able to build an entire way of practice because they broke those rules. They did not feel confined and restricted by what lawyers do to maintain their professional reputations and carved out a reputation of their own.

"That is, lawyers who fight to the end to defend their clients and that are never deterred by hopeless cases."

Photo by Ali Haider

 ## Sarah's Advice to her Daughters

When Sarah's two daughters pick their careers, she doesn't expect them to be lawyers, despite the fact that she believes one might be an excellent lawyer. She expects that whatever they do, it should include the idea of doing something that benefits humanity. That it should be at the center of it. She would be disappointed if their work did not include an aspect of that.

"I think it is very important to consider what you want to achieve out of your job. Decency and a dedicated life. To have some sort of goal of making the world a better place. You don't necessarily have to do a Ph.D. to make a lasting impact in the world, but ask yourself what your legacy is?"

Sarah on Breaking the Rules

Sarah is working in a system that was instinctively hostile to newcomers – and doubly so if they were female. During one of her first cases in Pakistan, she was up against a very brilliant and famous criminal lawyer who found it very amusing to have two women as opposing counsel. She wore the uniform men wear to court, not the one women wear to court. *"Sometimes, I don't look the part but that's what I felt comfortable in,"* she recalls.

The lawyer was sitting across from Sarah and hadn't done any preparation after hearing that there was a female, 20-something year old defense lawyer. He wanted to unnerve her before the judge came into the room. He turned to his associate and said, *"You know these barristers who come from fancy, fancy England with their fancy education? All they are good for is having these neat files,"* because Sarah had a pile of neat folders with her, *"But they don't really understand anything about this system,"* he continued.

"I remember just counting to ten and thinking - do not react," Sarah recalls. *"I am proud to say we kicked his butt and won."*

To learn more about Justice Project Pakistan www.jpp.org.pk or follow Sarah @ LinkedIn / SarahBelal

AUTHENTIC LIFE DESIGN

PERSONAL PURPOSE

We have gone through "Bold Change", we have considered how society today impacts us and the tools available to "Rock your Comfort Zone".

Now we will embark on **A** and **"Authentic Life Design"**. The importance of being true to yourself and defining what your personal purpose looks like for you.

At the end of this chapter, you will have drafted your personal purpose with the Becoming Queen Bee Exercise™ and defined the actions needed to get there. You will start by analyzing what you want to prioritize and define the goals aligned with that purpose. You will learn to break it down into actions that are needed in order to get there.

The scope of someone's individual purpose varies. We are all dealt with different hands in the game. We have different backgrounds, experiences, skills, and opportunities which affect our playfield. However, we are going to focus on where you have the power of influence, and ignore the rest. By weighing every passion and dream, you will be able to live an authentic life based on your desires. Nothing is right or wrong. It's about being you, and fulfilling your own expectations, using your personal circumstances and gifts. To define your purpose to allow you to be the best person you can be. You will not compete but instead, leverage your uniqueness.

Many of us struggle with a basic understanding of purpose. A personal purpose defines who you are and how you aspire to live your life. It is based on your passions and values, and it is reflected in your words, actions, behaviors, and decisions.

*"To give life meaning one must have
a purpose larger than oneself."*
- Will Durant

The exercise to define your purpose is the sole most important self-exploration you have to do in life. The foundation of bravery will help you realize it. A well-drafted purpose will make life much easier for you and provide clarity, relief, and fulfillment as you go along. It provides you with a compass in life - Something you can cling to when feeling lost and something that guides you in the right direction.

**A purpose provides you with a compass when
you feel lost or have to make life-changing decisions.**

Having worked in the corporate world defining strategic frameworks for corporations, I am surprised that so many people have not considered their own strategic direction. A direction based on the question of what sort of life to live. What do you want to be remembered for? Did you contribute to society at large? Did you make family your priority? Did you focus on being an accomplished professional?

So why are you curious to explore your personal purpose? Maybe you aren't or you didn't know you were. Maybe you just liked the book cover, got it as a gift, or just want to follow the authors' journey. It doesn't matter, we are grateful you are here.

Let's assume you might have felt some of the below:

✓ Trapped and disempowered?

✓ Overwhelmed and fed up with your current situation?

✓ Lost without a clear purpose?

✓ Demotivated and unseen in the world?

✓ Not 100% content - destined for more?

We believe you are a person who wants to optimize your life and make sure you are organized and heading in the right direction. You are ready to put in the work to create an improved life.

By exploring your personal purpose, you will:

✓ Gain empowerment, strength, and clarity to dare to take the leap you want

✓ Create an action list to take you where you want to go

✓ Make a big impact in the world like you are meant to do

✓ Break free from a structure that slowly kills your creativity and passion

Your personal purpose is similar to how a corporation looks at a vision. Consider how much time and money corporations spend, together with experts, to define what they are steering towards and what it means as a corporation.

"A vision is a mental picture of the result you want to achieve - a picture so clear and strong it will help make that result real."
- Johan Graham[6]

Having a vision provides a sense of purpose and direction for the business. It is well known that a business without a sense of direction minimizes the chances to reach its goals. The same goes for your life. The thought that most people don't go through the exercise of drafting their vision, also known as, their personal purpose, is a bit sad. Especially, since it doesn't have to take that much of an effort.

CREATE YOUR OWN

Uncovering the layers of what is important to you is a lifelong process. Once you have created your purpose you will go back and tweak and refine it often. The purpose is based on the core of what is important to you.

Realize that there is no minimum level of impact your purpose should have. It is entirely up to you what your purpose might be. A personal purpose might be life-changing, or it might just be about adding some elements to your life which have been missing. If you have decided that you want to pursue your passion for climbing, you should find your gut and the tools to go after it. If you find it important to spend more time with your children, prioritize it and make it happen. If a career is most important for you, define what is needed to get there and go for it.

Never compare and never look down on someone else's purpose. However, other's personal purpose statements might give you inspiration. And you could help inspire others by sharing your own.

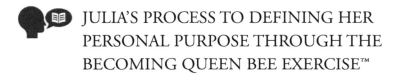 JULIA'S PROCESS TO DEFINING HER PERSONAL PURPOSE THROUGH THE BECOMING QUEEN BEE EXERCISE™

As an illustration on how to create your own personal purpose, we will follow fictional Julia's reasoning to define her purpose. Let her story serve as a guideline for you.

Julia stepped into the hallway to her two-bedroom recently renovated apartment in Amsterdam. The day had been long. In irritation, she threw her Manolo Blahnik shoes towards the shoe rack. This day was not a good day indeed. Her boss had told her that there was no way she could be promoted this year within the company. Apparently, she had reached the top of the hierarchy.

She just wanted to cry - life felt so meaningless. Earlier this year she had turned 38 years old, and she had been feeling a lack of direction. She loved her job and had worked hard to become Partner and Director at a well-known communication firm in the city.

She slides into her favorite pajamas, brings out a frozen dinner, and pours herself a glass of wine. She was lucky, she had everything, didn't she? Lately, she had the nagging feeling that something was missing in her life, however, she could not figure out what it was.

She had considered if it was a lack of "meaning in life", but she thought it sounded like something spoiled brats explore when lacking useful things to do.

"I am really not a spoiled brat. I have always worked hard for everything I have. I did everything expected from me and more. I was a top performer at university and spent most of the time studying. I was quite boring and should probably have enjoyed my student years more. I had wisely placed a small heritage into buying an apartment and my long hours building my career had allowed me to pay off my mortgage. I was quite proud of my current achievements, what could be missing in my life - a purpose, a meaning, a plan?"

While enjoying a portion of frozen lasagna she started to consider what was important in life.
"My family, of course, I love them dearly."

Julia had a close bond with her parents who lived quite close by and up until recently she used to go there every Sunday for dinner. However, when she came to think about it, that hadn't happened for a while. Her sister and two children used to come too. Her two nieces adored her, and she loved them. If she remembered correctly, her sister had asked her to be their godmother at some point. *"What actually is the duty of a godmother?"* She probably hadn't really taken the task seriously whatever that duty is. *"I shouldn't forget to give them some gifts next time"*.

Considering a family of her own felt hopeless. She had been on Tinder but the quality there was below acceptable. She had wasted so many good weekends stuck on awkward dates and at some point, she told herself enough is enough, to keep her sanity. That was almost three years ago. *"Had it really been years?!"*

She really wanted to meet someone though. Like really, really, really. Most of her friends had disappeared into the suburbs with kids and a husband. That traditional lifestyle scared her, but she was pretty sure she wanted to have kids of her own one day.

Oh, what a depressing night. Sitting here alone considering what the purpose of life is.

"Maybe I should just continue watching Netflix. The thought of purpose intrigued her though. *"I guess '****Family****' is the highest priority for me now,"* she thinks to herself as she scribbles it down on the back of an envelope.

Her thoughts wander back to the irritating conversation with her boss. *"What did she mean 'no chance for promotion'? Insane, what was the whole purpose then, willing to give the company the best years of her life and this is all they would offer her."*

It wasn't an option to change jobs, she loved her workplace. She and the team had so much fun and the clients they worked with were fun, well-known brands. How can Partner and Director be at the top of the hierarchy? Anger and disappointment rushed through her body. Maybe she was left with no choice, maybe she had to switch jobs. Or maybe her title was just a title. The salary had been going up and there were other ways of achieving something. Even though right now she had a hard time picturing what that would be. She needed a side project which brought her joy and where she could channel some of her passion.

She spent way too much time watching Netflix, time that could be used wiser. She writes "explore **self-achievement**" in big letters next to **"family"**.

"Where had all her friends gone lately?" She used to love hanging out with her girlfriends, they can't all have disappeared to the suburbs. She knew at least five women who were still single - they must be doing all this fun stuff without her. She had been horrible with her social life lately. Prioritizing work and the whole "work, dinner, Netflix" life she had created made her rather depressed. Being **"social"** is definitely important to her.

✓ Family ✓ Self Achievement ✓ Social

"I guess prioritizing family is something I will do, while I am pursuing self-achievement in a social environment. Spending too much time alone not only makes me talk to myself, it is also dangerously depressing. I guess my purpose would be:

Prioritizing family while pursuing self-achievement combined with a social life."

"Not sure a professional life coach would accept this, but good enough for now. This whole little exercise made me feel better already. At least I know what is important to me. It only took a little over an hour and an exquisite glass of Cabernet Sauvignon, but why didn't I do this before?"

It's one thing to know what you want, but the question is how to achieve it.

"I guess I want children at some point, but I can't force myself on more Tinder dates. Is it only me or are there many weird men on Tinder?"

The last date was over a coffee, easier to end than over wine, and we met in a hotel lobby. He was ten minutes late - people who don't respect other people's time are just plain rude. He had the tiniest hands she had ever seen. Not small hands but really, really tiny. A second date with that man was out of the question.

She knew she had to put an effort into actively meeting someone. Someone at work had mentioned another App, apparently it is more selective. She could try that one. And didn't Lottie at work also suggest she had a suitable blind date for her? She had probably just laughed it away.

"Who had time for blind dates, and did Lottie really know her type anyway? Maybe she should have tried? I could do one date every second week."

For a moment she wanted to increase the ambition level to once a week, but that was probably just unrealistic. For someone who hadn't been on a date in over two years, this was a big step.

"When I come to think of it, I shouldn't have to force myself to find a man, just because I want children. Technology today gives me new possibilities and I could do it on my own. It's not the ultimate scenario but it's an option. I know at least two colleagues who did IVF on their own. The thought had been in the back of my head for a long time, but I had always pushed it aside. From what I heard, it's a rather complicated and long process which is a reason to explore what it is all about in a good time. To pursue the goal of a family I would have to:

✓ *Explore the process of IVF*

✓ *Probably save for the process - what could it cost??*

✓ *Download the most sophisticated competitor to Tinder*

✓ *Go on one date every second week*

✓ *Be open to blind dates*

Exhausting this thing.

Concerning self-achievement, I don't really know where to start, and what does it even mean? It's about achieving something I've challenged myself to do. I should probably choose something I am really good at if I should have a fair chance to become really famous and successful. But I assume it should be something I do for myself and fame and success are not the end goal. I guess not, but it wouldn't hurt, would it?"

"As a 12-year-old, I was the best writer in my class. My teacher loved me and on the days we had to write essays, I arrived excited at school. I am not really sure if I ever used that passion. I guess that is what led me into communication, but honestly, not much writing these days. My days are usually filled with meetings, brainstorming, and coffee - a lot of coffee. Could my self-fulfillment project be to write a book? Is it slightly ridiculous, to picture myself as an author? I hope it's not the wine speaking, everyone would probably draw the conclusion I have a 'turning 40' crisis. I am not sure when I started to care so much about other people's thoughts though."

"Today you can become your own publisher, you can publish your book online and it would be printed on-demand. My sister could help me design my book cover, she is a brilliant art director, and the cover must be stunning. This is actually fun! I think I should go for it. I could even crowdfund it for good PR and fame."

"In that case, I would need to:

✓ *Explore what kind of book I want to write*

✓ *Draft the outline*

✓ *Set aside time to write - one evening a week and Sundays*

✓ *Find a self-publishing site, meet my sister to brainstorm the cover, find a proof-reader at Fiverr*

✓ *Explore crowdfunding*

"Don't tell anyone I am writing a book - I don't want to jinx it and prefer just showing up at the next family gathering with 'Author' on my business card.

The only goal left now is to take control of my social life. A hard task to solve since I have been upright antisocial lately - not sure how it came to this. Hope some friends are left in the city and remember me - I wouldn't blame them if they didn't. The ones in the suburbs are long gone. Apparently, you are frightening to small children as a single, child-free woman, so those dinner invitations just never came. I didn't care too much since I couldn't think of a more depressing way to spend an evening. Maybe on a Tinder date."

"There must be some fun friends left. I might have seen some on Facebook a while ago. There have also been a number of after-work drinks invitations at work, politely declined due to Netflix. I always thought that as a boss I probably should keep some distance. I certainly haven't made it easy for myself. No, I need to do something. Easter is in a month, which would be the perfect excuse to arise from the dead and invite a nice crowd to dinner. From now on, I'll be better, and I will take every opportunity to socialize. I will:

✓ *Continuously explore social opportunities*

✓ *Attend after-work drinks*

✓ *Join a book writing circle - @ MeetUp there are events on every subject, it might even be an alternative to meet someone*

✓ *Visit my family more often, and embrace my duty as godmother - can't believe I had forgotten about that"*

"It's already 11.30 P.M. - I need to go to bed and sleep on all this. I feel amazing, this could be my roadmap for the years to come, and I did it all alone without a psychologist or life coach leading me into this direction. The funny thing is that the answers were there all the time, within me. I guess I just hadn't taken the time or asked myself the right questions."

"That night I went to sleep exhausted but happy. I felt a sense of accomplishment already. This will be fun and if the book project fails - at least I tried."

That was Julia's reasoning while drafting her personal purpose. Based on similar reasoning, you will now be doing the Becoming Queen Bee Exercise™ in three different steps:

1.) IDENTIFY PASSION POINTS

2.) DRAFT PERSONAL PURPOSE

3.) DEFINE ACTIONS

Next to the tasks, you will be reminded what Julia put down as an example.

IDENTIFY PASSION POINTS

The first stage of the process is not a hard thing to do. The risk is that perfection and over-analysis will halt this process. Remember that your personal purpose is not a static statement. It is organic and changes with life itself: You change your mind, you might have fulfilled some parts, or you have more important aspects which you want to include.

My guess is that you haven't taken enough time to reflect upon life and meaning, and the overarching ingredients that are important to you. My first time visualizing my passions was in my late 30s during a self development course. When you are younger you are more risk-prone and you have less to lose so the earlier you explore your purpose the better.

As we know, life often takes us on a journey, and we don't have time to take control of the steering wheel. We end up just riding along, keeping a fast grip to not fall off. You have to compromise to make life work. Therefore, it is important to go back to your childhood to remember your purest dreams without interference.

To go back to what the dreamer and child in you value.

If you are a parent, it is easy to put these dreams into your child's future instead. To imagine that your child is the one who should achieve all those things you dreamt about. Please don't exclude yourself from the equation. By leading by example, you will serve as an inspiration for your child, and it is never too late to pursue a passion.

Big or small, no right or wrong. It could be something you want to happen or an overarching focus area you want to prioritize in life which means something to you.

Which values do you prioritize? What is your ideal set-up? What would you do if you had the time? What is break free for you/purpose/passion? What is important to you? What were your dreams as a child? What do you want to happen right now? What do you feel needs to change in your life?

Examples:

Passion/Love

- find love
- projects (write a book, paint, cook)

Family

- more time
- create one

Friends/Social

- maintain
- prioritize
- develop friendship

Freedom

- flexibility
- live in the countryside
- travel
- change of location

Career

- excel at work
- change
- entrepreneurship / start a business

Self-Realization/Purpose/Achievement

- explore passion or project (give back to society / pursue a hobby)
- accomplishment (climb a mountain, write a book)
- change (divorce / break-up / marriage)
- meaning (at work, in general)

Wellness / Health

- improve (be fit)
- focus/prioritize on health/wellness (food, sleep, fun/more leisure time)
- mental wellbeing (meditation, mental challenge, spirituality)

Education

- personal development (courses)
- explore / curiosity

Time

- good habits

- structure/prioritize

Here you might put down "spend more quality time with my daughter" but identify and scribble down the overarching word for this is: "*Family*". If you start with the feeling that "*I need to change work, it needs to have purpose*" you should put down: "*Meaningful work*". If you feel that you need to "*Stop running and start living*", the way to reach that goal would be more freedom and flexibility so put down "*Flexibility*".

 IDENTIFY YOUR PASSION POINTS!

Write down the most important aspects of your life where you feel an urge to focus. For inspiration go back and review your dreams under Bold Change. Write down a maximum of ten, but more likely between three to five. Remember, many can be refined and clustered under one overarching point.

In order to clear your thoughts, a mind map is a useful tool. Firstly, start with you as the central point. From there, list your priorities and categorize them around the overarching passion point as in the example below. This exercise helps you become more structured and clearly visualize the areas that are important to you.

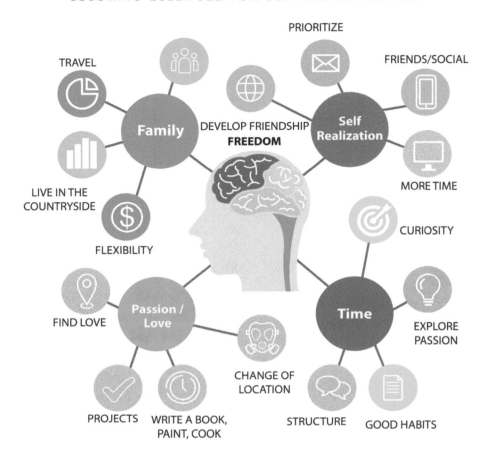

Your Passion Points	Julia's Example
1.)	1. Family
2.)	2. Self-achievement
3.)	3. Social life
4.)	
5.)	

Don't panic, this is just the first step: Brainstorming. This is something that you can revisit.

DRAFT PERSONAL PURPOSE

Now we will take these passion points to create your Personal Purpose based on your passion points. It needs to be rather short for you to remember it and it should be broad enough not to limit you. It has to be aligned with your core values and it has to be an overall goal of how you want to live your life. Remember that there are many levels of purpose tweaked towards career, personal development, lifestyle, and family depending on where you are in your life and what is important to you now.

Examples:

EMPHASIZE MEANING

"I serve others as a visionary leader and apply ethical principles in management to make a significant difference in the world."

EMPHASIZE CAREER

"My purpose is to inspire others and flourish financially as a speaker, writer, and entrepreneur."

EMPHASIZE SELF FULLFILLMENT

"I want to live a global free, passionate life and build value for the future."

EMPHASIZE FAMILY AND MEANING

"I want to be a good mother to my children and make sure my job gives me meaning for myself and others."

EMPHASIZE FAMILY AND SOCIAL

"Prioritize family while pursuing self-achievement combined with a social life."

It is easy to get stuck here for the reasons we have mentioned earlier in the book: fear, priorities and expectations. Beware of the devil on your left shoulder whispering, *"You are not twenty anymore and can't become a hippie, living off nothing"*.

Your right devil counters with, *"There is something called a Nomad Capitalist Lifestyle. There is not only one way of 'working' – I would achieve much more if I were inspired."*

Don't listen to any of them. Remember, the importance of living true to yourself. Right now, we want to know your inner wishes. You are defining what your heart is dreaming about, and then we will go through what it takes to get there, and if it is reasonable and worth pursuing - A potential game plan. But it is important that you don't kill this process because that is what most people do when they get this far, and that is why they never pursue their personal purpose.

 DRAFT YOUR PERSONAL PURPOSE

Include the most essential information based on your passion points. Draft something. Anything.

Don't worry. You will revisit and tweak this drafted purpose on a regular basis.

My Personal Purpose	Julia's Personal Purpose
	"Prioritizing family while pursuing self-achievement in a social environment."

Prioritizing family while pursuing self-achievement in a social environment

DRAFT PERSONAL PURPOSE

CREATE ACTION PLAN

Now we will break down your personal purpose and explore what is needed to pursue it. We will create a roadmap. Perhaps you have put down "Freedom" as an important aspect in your life. This feels worth pursuing. A sense of freedom could mean many things: flexibility, a dream to live in the countryside, a dream to travel more, or to work for yourself. It could also be based on a feeling such as feeling trapped and stuck in a boring, restrictive routine.

Take a moment and define what freedom means to you and what is needed to achieve that in your life. What you are aiming for might be life-changing, but it could also be your priorities. For example:

- Put aside an hour a week to pursue your own project

- Become an entrepreneur or freelancer

- Start planning for a life abroad

- Schedule travel with the family

 DEFINE ACTIONS

Below you will list the actions that will help you achieve your Personal Purpose. Consider your strengths and your uniqueness. This plan will of course be tweaked and modified as life goes on.

YOUR PERSONAL PURPOSE:

_____

_____

_____

JULIA'S PERSONAL PURPOSE:

*"Prioritizing **family** while pursuing **self-achievement** in a **social** environment."*

Your Passion Point 1:	Julia's Passion Point 1: FAMILY
ACTION	ACTION
	✓ Explore the process of IVF
	✓ Probably save for the process - what could it cost??
	✓ Download the most sophisticated competitor to Tinder
	✓ Go on one date every second week
	✓ Be open for blind dates

These very reasonable tasks are quite achievable for Julia and she will probably be able to tick them off quickly. Then she will be able to add some more or keep the long-term ones on there.

Your Passion Point 2:	Julia's Passion Point 2: SELF-ACHIEVEMENT
	✓ Explore what kind of book I want to write
	✓ Draft the outline
	✓ Set aside time to write - one evening a week and Sundays
	✓ Find the self-publishing site, meet my sister to brainstorm the cover, find a proof-reader at Fiverr
	✓ Explore crowdfunding

This is a project which will help Julia explore her passion and challenge herself. It will probably not take more than one to two years to achieve, and it will teach her a lot and give her a sense of achievement. If she fails, at least she tried and hopefully she learned something in the process.

Your Passion Point 3:	Julia's Passion Point 3: SOCIAL
	✓ Continuously explore social opportunities
	✓ Attend after-work drinks at work
	✓ Join a book writing circle - @ MeetUp there are events on every subject, it might even be an alternative to meet someone
	✓ Visit my family more often, and embrace my duty as godmother - can't believe I had forgotten about that

This is a behavioral change that she might remove once she has changed the behavior to be more social. If she feels she needs to be reminded and that it is such an important part of her purpose, she can include it long-term.

Explore what kind of book I want to write ;

Draft the outline ;

Set aside time to write-one evening a week and Sundays ;

Find a self-publishing site, brainstorm cover with designer and find a proof-reader at Fiverr;

Explore crowdfounding;

Congratulations you have now defined your personal purpose and you have an action list to achieve it.

Review your personal purpose on New Year's Eve every year and see what you have achieved and what you want to modify. Feel free to do a personal purpose together with your partner if that feels right. To have a common goal as a couple is a great way to work together and experience unity in your relationship.

Keep it close to you, reflect on it, and tweak it. Let it change, but keep it as a companion throughout life.

"The two most important days in your life are the day you are born, and the day you find out why."
- Mark Twain

Share your purpose on www.queenbeecolony.com to inspire others.

INSPIRATION - DRAFT
PERSONAL PURPOSE

PERSONAL STORY: AUTHOR ELIN WIBELL

My Personal Purpose

My journey started after a leadership training that I didn't want to attend. Follow how I started to pursue a Personal Purpose and my reasoning behind it.

Photo by Frida Marklund

I worked in a corporate structure for eleven years. We did a lot of work defining visions for corporations. One day I was invited to attend a Seven Habits training at work. While sitting there we learned many useful tools such as the importance of carrying our weather within, and not being affected by external demotivators we couldn't control. We also briefly touched upon the importance of considering what is important to me as a person. I remember thinking that many in this course might be realizing that they should probably change jobs and that it was generous of the company to take the risk of losing employees.

Maybe it wasn't generous. Maybe both the corporation and you benefit from that - you stay true to yourself and the business has the right person in the right position.

After that day I started questioning my current situation. I loved my job - it was actually really fun - and I had great colleagues. I got to work with sustainability which I loved. I thought that I could easily stay in the company for the rest of my life, but deep inside, I knew it was time to move on. There was more I needed to do. I didn't know exactly what, but I knew I had to try to figure it out.

Suddenly, my life changed in every direction. I broke off an eleven-year relationship. We sold our mutual apartment and I felt completely lost.

"It is often when you change one thing that other changes follow. It is hard to explain, and nothing you can predict, but it often occurs."

One day, when I lived as a single woman in a temporarily rented apartment, I found myself hesitantly walking over to my cousin's birthday party. Amongst the celebrating relatives, I suddenly saw one of their friends, a man that I had met before in life, but when circumstances were not in our favor to pursue something romantic.

Long story short, after a rowdy afterparty at my cousin's, we became a couple. The same year, we did our first vacation together on a cruise ship in Hawaii. Yes, cruise ships are mainly for nearly deads and newlyweds, but during one evening on the balcony, we found the time to draft our common personal purpose. It wasn't a great ritual where we analyzed every aspect of our lives. We simply talked about what we thought was important in life and what kind of life we wanted to live. We started to scribble on a napkin. We started with what we value in life and then what we needed to achieve it. With the same simple 3-step method used in the Becoming Queen Bee Exercise™.

We have followed the personal purpose we defined as a couple that same night until this day, tweaking it every now and then. It has helped us tremendously when we have felt lost or had to make a choice between A or B.

Firstly, our purpose was to have a "global free life". After consideration, we know that many people do this as hippies living on the beach, settling down anywhere, taking low paid jobs. This is perfectly fine, but this was not for us. We wanted to refine our vision further. We love business and we love our careers, and we were not willing to trade down our lifestyle. Having well-paid jobs and enjoying the comforts of that were important to us, so we included "A non-cheap passionate life" and "while building value for the future."

Now our vision is:

"To live a global free, non-cheap, passionate life while building value for the future."

Global has always been an important part of both our lives and something we both value. We want to be able to travel and have flexibility in where we live. Therefore, our aim is to have flexible careers working from a distance. The possibility to explore alternative revenue streams such as property investments for rental, stocks and freelancing, has also been beneficial.

However, being "free" also comes with a feeling of rootlessness so we want to build value to the future with a "base" where we will be able to have a home.

After much consideration, we have now found that home in Spain. It will allow us to have a base, but it can also be something we invest in and rent out while living in other places.

Personally, separate from our couple's purpose, I have spent a lot of time and energy exploring my professional passions. I have created an App for LGBTQ+ traveling, I have started Social Good Agency to work with CSR, and I have engaged in start-ups which I believe are contributing to society at large.

We believe that this will guide us for the next five years, but we will revise it when needed. Now we measure everything against our vision, without being static about it. Sometimes the goals might change the vision. There is something in your subconscious which guides you and by being able to articulate it, you live true to yourself.

Vulnerable Expression

Bold Change will help you **R**ock your Comfort Zone. You have defined your personal purpose for an **A**uthentic Life Design. Now we will go through **V**ulnerable Expression, how it affects you, and how you can handle what comes with it.

It is inevitable that you become more vulnerable by daring to follow your passions. You are putting your heart on your sleeve and people will judge something that might feel quite private.

I remember when I left my stable set-up, people were puzzled about how that could work for me. Critical questions surrounding salary and work ethics arose, *"No, I will not be free to meet every time you sneak out earlier from the office"*. This combined with a mother who thinks you can only work from an office, I constantly felt like I needed to defend and explain my personal choices. This could perhaps be a reason why many hesitate to go outside the norm, simply because being questioned and showing vulnerability is draining.

"Remembering that you are going to die is the
best way I know to avoid the trap of thinking
you have something to lose. You are already naked.
There is no reason not to follow your heart."
- Steve Jobs

There are many aspects around vulnerability. It might be that you are not coping well with being questioned, that you listen too much to other people's opinions, or that you are afraid to be judged or fail. In that case, it becomes much more comfortable to not do anything. But that is not an option if you want to dare to live life to the fullest. So, let's analyze how you can deal with what vulnerability brings and stay strong and on course with your purpose.

By being brave you put your chin out there which means anxiety, hurdles, and fears will most likely follow. There are many different ways to cope with these side effects and you have to find the solutions that work in your favor. My mother, who is a very wise person, always encouraged me to embrace when I felt down. That without moments of despair and anxiety, there would be no highs. I always try to remember that. Like most people, when I realize that a project might not work out, I tend to initially feel a huge disappointment in myself - questioning my abilities and choices. But then I take a deep breath and put my faith in the fact that when this has passed, my luck will return.

I have also come to realize that a project might feel doomed but then suddenly a breakthrough happens due to hard work and external changes around it, which I might not have anticipated. The key is to keep the vision and not to panic. It could be that this project is sleeping for a year and then suddenly there is the momentum you've been waiting for.

Don't forget the advice we got from the majority of the interviews we've done: The importance of dividing the project, or the problem, into small actions or manageable chunks. By doing this, whether it is a problem or a project, it doesn't seem quite as hard to handle. This will also help to diminish the anxiety around it.

You also have to be kind to yourself. Pat yourself on the shoulder and remind yourself how far you have come and what you have done right. Try to focus on your achievements so far.

Another aspect is that it is difficult to drive a passion without the structure of office hours. This could also be the case when having a routine job and then try to manage a passion project on the side. Some people find this extremely difficult and suffer from it. Some good advice when you don't feel the energy, is to actually just take a break. Focus on something else that day. Come back when you feel energized. Passion projects are very much based on energy and therefore it is alright to await that energy. If the days pass and the energy doesn't seem to come, try to do mundane tasks where less energy is needed. Create your own routines by making sure you are clearing your head with exercise or find inspiration through conferences, books or meetings. Here it is also extremely important to be kind to yourself and give yourself the right tools. If you need an office to focus, rent one. If you need a break that day, take one.

There is also a lot of good to gain from showing vulnerability. By sharing moments of vulnerability, you are building trust with others. You are more likely to find solutions and handle your anxiety or problem. When anxious, it often helps to talk about it. You often figure out it's not as scary as it was portrayed in your head. By talking about it you are able to find solutions to your problem. We are not talking oversharing in a professional environment but with your trusted group of supporters. However, some vulnerabilities could be useful to share in a professional environment. By showing vulnerability you show strength through courage and people will connect with you on a human level and that creates trust.

TOXIC PEOPLE / CARRY
YOUR WEATHER WITHIN

Since pursuing your passions is still considered quite unconventional among many, you have to expect to be questioned by others besides you questioning yourself. There are many reasons others will have opinions about your decisions. Some might be worried about you. Some might be jealous and by questioning you, they might justify why they are not doing it themselves.

If you go down the entrepreneurial path, you have to be prepared to get your idea questioned and most likely hear that it has been done before. When I first started to talk about the mobile application I was developing, I received countless links to similar services. This might not be a bad thing, it is good to keep track of the market. However, you are most likely to have done the research yourself and it might not be relevant.

Appreciate opinions, but make sure they are valid. If you act on all "good advice" you will probably end up doing nothing or with a project that is nothing like you envisioned. You have to learn to trust yourself and do your own audit of your idea. Learn to be strong and keep your course without listening too much to others.

It is also important to be aware of other people's intentions. Unfortunately, many feel self-achievement by putting others down. Don't let it get to you and never apologize for being a woman, junior or senior for that matter.

In Northern European countries, we have something called the "Law of Jante" - a mindset that no one should think they are better than the other. This is a code of conduct based on the common good and the collective. This could be a true barrier for exploring yourself. If someone puts you down, keep this Law of Jante in mind. It is especially applicable when you are trying to do things out of the ordinary or showing individuality or personal ambition. "You are not to believe you are smarter / better / know more / can teach us anything". There is no reason to be apologetic, miss out on what you want to do, or not stand your ground.

During your life, you will stumble upon people who put others down to flourish themselves. We could call them toxic people. Some of them are fully aware and use this tactic to feel better and some are causing hurt and anger without even noticing it. Whatever the reason, it is of utmost importance that you are able to recognize this behavior and learn how to deal with it. Save your time and energy for what you want to achieve in life instead.

"Great minds discuss ideas, average ones discuss events, and small minds discuss people."
- Eleanor Roosevelt

So instead of having your buttons pushed, recognize this behavior and create a tactic for how you want to handle it. I would like to highlight the method of Franklin Covey, who was a world leader in coaching human behavior, which is to "Carry Your Own Weather".

This reasoning is very helpful and has been adopted by many. Neurologist Victor Frankl famously said, "Between stimulus and response there is a space. In that space is our power to choose our response. In our response lies our growth and our freedom." This is mindfulness in a nutshell. Even if you are high on anxiety and short on time, you can claim the space in between.[7]

So, whether you call it "Carry Your Own Weather" or "Mindfulness" the rationale behind it is that you have space between stimulus and response, and you should claim that space and have the freedom to choose your response.

External distractions like mean co-workers, lack of resources or bad luck will always happen in your life. The key is how you decide to react to it. Picture a rainy day, where you are deciding to appreciate the spring rain showering you on your way home. You could have been irritated but instead, it is making you feel alive. This is carrying your own weather.

In a more confrontational setting, you can decide to react immediately and let anger, frustration and disappointment flush over you. But this will most likely lead to resentment, stress, unhappiness, and dejection. Or you can take a moment and decide how you want to act on this. Don't get emotionally triggered or victimized. You have a choice on how you will respond.

"Between what happens to us and how we react to what happens to us is a space. In that space lies our freedom and power to choose."
- Dr. Stephen R. Covey

For specific "problems" heading your way, there are also many other tools you can use. Say for example you have a co-worker who constantly puts you down or questions your decisions. An easy way to deal with this could be to distance yourself from this person. This might not be possible, but at least you can try to limit your interactions. You can also set him/her aside as a "psychology project" and try different methods for smooth interactions. Try to beat them with facts and reasoning, and don't get caught in their emotional drama. When you are triggered emotionally, it's easy to forget that you have a choice as to how to respond. Take a deep breath and take a moment.

TOXIC PEOPLE

 PERSONAL STORY - AUTHOR ELIN WIBELL

How to Handle Rude People - Carry Your Own Weather

Fresh out of University, I am stressed to impress at my new work, but I am taken away by a quick insult. Or was it a joke?

I had just got my first job in the industry in which I really wanted to work. I felt like I had won the lottery. I was quite shy and a bit taken by the fact that I was now working in a huge international corporation. I wanted to show them that I was worthy all the time and I always spent the longest hours in the office in front of my computer. I had decided that I was always going to be the last one to leave the office. With the notion that this is what all high performers do, I was very much trapped by social pressure.

One day a consultant we had worked with for years was in our office. After a full day of meetings, my boss, him and I wrapped it up. I finished the conversation by saying, "Is there anything else I can help with?" I was always quite polite and had an exaggerated respectful tone and approach towards seniors. I blame it on my years in boarding school. He turned around and said, "Yes, you can polish my shoes".

As most people admit when these kinds of insults happen at work, I didn't manage to say something snappy in return and I just laughed it off. This could have been an attempt of some kind of domination technique from his side or maybe just a bad joke.

Either way it was not a nice thing to say to an insecure, junior in a professional environment. Unfortunately, being in a social environment you have to be prepared for clashes and rudeness at times. This can often happen at work as a competitive environment. Remember to always carry your weather within - don't let it affect you. If you are able to do that, you are able to show that it doesn't affect you. Also, remember that you are able to behave differently yourself and as a role model when you are the more senior person.

VULNERABLE EXPRESSION

 PERSONAL STORY - AUTHOR MARIE FALKENBERG

When Life Pushes You Down and You Have to Find Your Purpose Again

A break-up turned my world upside down and took me into a deep depression. It became one of these moments when you think the despair will never leave.

Years ago, I started dating my love from university with whom I always had a special bond. We always looked up to each other, we were best friends, we were great travel buddies, and we shared the same interests and friends. I moved to his home country and we quickly started to plan our future. Our relationship was effortless and fun, and I had never felt that kind of love and pure happiness before.

After years, like a flash from a clear sky and without a proper explanation, he broke up with me, leaving me devastated and confused.

"I felt so much pain, a pain that I am not even able to express. I could hardly move."

For at least a year and a half, I was in and out of the hospital due to severe suffering from panic attacks. I was not able to breathe, and I thought that I was going to die from it many times over. I used to lay in bed at night and feel my legs running. It was impossible to sleep, and I kept on getting up in the middle of the night during completely random hours to walk and swallow beta-blockers to calm my anxiety. For those of you who have suffered from panic attacks, I am sure you know very well how awful the feeling is.

I walked for hours and I never felt tired from it. I lost about 15 kg in those first six months. The minute I stopped walking, all those hopeless feelings kept showering over me, and I felt like I did not want to stay in this life anymore. I started having suicidal thoughts but at the same time, I knew I would not act on them as I understood that the exact mood I was in will pass. Things felt so hopeless, so stupid, and so pointless, and I felt hatred towards myself as well as towards others.

For a long time, I was stuck in bed crying, with no appetite, and with panic attacks coming regularly. My whole career and life, that I fought so hard to get, collapsed; I just could not see the point of anything anymore. I had moved back in with my parents as I was not able to look after myself.

I was not able to function or to think clearly. I went to several therapists, but unfortunately, nothing helped. I was stuck in severe depression. It took me years to recover and finally with time, I felt the willingness to live again.

It does not mean that the memories or the disappointment and anger were gone, but I had learnt how to live with them and to control them. It took me close to five years to feel that I was ready for another romantic relationship. Even though I wanted it to happen sooner, nothing worked. A lot of it was due to me not being ready. I knew I wanted to show another side of myself, but the pain and disappointment were still too visible.

During this time, I felt so powerless in my situation. Trust me, this was a very unusual feeling for me. People around me saw me as an extremely strong person who could handle anything. This severe sadness made people around me feel desperate - whatever they did or said could not make me feel better. However, after some time when I had no more tears to cry, something happened. I told myself that I had two options. Option one was to jump out of the window, and the second option was to try and find the purpose of my life again. Luckily, I chose option two.

What this experience has taught me is that life is a rollercoaster that can really go up and down. Not just down but steeply down. Whenever you feel severe pain or when a traumatic experience happens to you, it teaches us a lot about ourselves and we learn things that we didn't even know we didn't know.

Additionally, it shows us clearly who our real friends are, and who truly cares for you. I have always been an extremely funny, slightly crazy, and adventurous person who people enjoyed being around. So, whenever this person exchanged for a depressed grey cloud who could not offer all that positive energy anymore, people turned away, and luckily for me some people stayed.

Your life and how you want to live is a choice and only your choice – make sure to make the most out of it and be grateful for the things and the people that you have by your side.

From such heart-breaking experiences, one thing that can be learned is that pain provides us with more compassion, empathy, and love. Pain can also bring you closer to one another and it will be easier to emphasize with another person when they feel in distress. However, having said this, I would not wish it upon anyone to feel the way I did.

 Remember to be happy about the person you are. Your happiness does not depend on others. Be brave and ask for help when you feel that you need it and stop to think that you need to take care of everything yourself. Let other people help you and guide you. Life does not always happen the way you want and plan it, however, it will be something else and perhaps something even better.

"There is a crack in everything.
That is how the lights get in."
- Leonard Cohen Anthem

 ## TAKE CONTROL OF YOUR FEARS

A helpful way to take control of your feelings is to list your fears and what triggers anxiety. By doing this it becomes less scary and by understanding your triggers you can start developing a new relationship with your anxiety. Remember that some anxiety is rational and helpful, and it can help you predict worse possible outcomes.

Anxiety / Problem	Fear / Trigger	Probable / Likely to happen	Action
1.			
2.			
3.			
4.			
5.			
6.			
7.			

You can handle large problems with small actions. Approach them slowly, bit by bit. By being proactive you minimize the risks and handle problems as they occur.

TO CONSIDER

✓ Embrace that the journey can be a struggle and stay calm during hard times. Have faith that highs will follow. Even though hard, the benefit of exploring your true self will not be a waste. By exploring who you truly are, you avoid spending your life searching.

✓ Even though it can be painful to get others' opinions on your project - appreciate valid feedback. You have your roadmap through your Personal Purpose when questioned. Remind yourself of your goal and stay on course.

✓ Don't be afraid to fail, it's part of the learning experience, and it's inevitable. Be kind to yourself and allow yourself a break when needed. Remember that unexpected breakthroughs often happen due to previous efforts.

✓ You can never really disconnect while you are pursuing your passion, because you don't really want to, so don't underestimate the importance of routines. Ensure a work/life balance and healthy habits, and give yourself the right prerequisites for success.

✓ Be aware of toxic people and choose how you respond to them - take the moment. When needed, ask for help whether it be from trusted friends or professionals.

Enjoy your Evolution

You have done the hard work and gone through what it means to be brave and to rock your comfort zone. To live closer to your true purpose and an authentic life. You have some tools to use and a clearer purpose and you know the road might not be easy but that there are methods to use. So why are we doing this? The purpose is of course, is to enjoy life. To feel satisfied and in control. So let's look at how kindness can improve our lives and how you can move from not only surviving but to thriving.

BENEFIT FROM THE ACT OF KINDNESS

We can't address enjoying life without first mentioning the benefit you get from the act of kindness. Who would have known that by doing good for others you are enriching your own life? A huge power lies in doing good. Being kind gives you a sense of validation. It makes you feel good. The more you give, the more you tend to get back from people. Some people see kindness as the great purpose of life itself.

Quite certainly there will be times when you are confronted by ethical dilemmas in life - where you have a split second to make an ethical decision. You might have to step in when a small child declines a birthday party because the little girl in her class is not cool enough, you might be asked to do something compromising at work, or you might have the choice to either be encouraging or judging.

Often these moments are popping up when you are quite unprepared and without you paying much attention to them. These times we instinctively adhere to our inner moral compass, our current mood, or gut feeling.

Despite maybe some psychopaths, we all have, to a certain degree, a built-in moral compass: Values we carry with us since upbringing, ideals we admire, and principles we live by.

However, it is unlikely that we will not make some poor decisions throughout life. Many successful people believe that there needs to be some kind of compromise done to achieve success, that some values or decisions have to be sacrificed. This in turn makes them assume that this would be the way to go: To sacrifice something to rise to the top. They often reflect this notion on junior co-workers or even their children without paying too much attention to it.

"I had to make some hard decisions, stepping on some toes and compromising my values to get where I am today, it is inevitable, it's the rule of the game."

This is something to be aware of and something unacceptable as the rule of the game. Just because some people make poor choices, it doesn't justify other people's poor choices. It is important to break out of that notion and follow your own moral compass at all times. Don't compromise morals and consider the positive benefits of being kind.

Moral compass: An inner sense which distinguishes what is right from what is wrong, functioning as a guide (like the needle of a compass) for morally appropriate behavior.
- Wikipedia

Did You Know That Kindness is Contagious?

You might think that your actions don't matter too much, but believe me, they do. Each person and their small acts of kindness matter. Always remember that we are all going through our own battles. The colleague who was rude to you at work might just have received the news that she has cancer. The clerk in the supermarket who didn't smile at you might be going through a divorce. The fact is, we can never know what is going on in someone's life. It is quite safe to assume that most people wouldn't behave badly if they felt good.

The benefit of the doubt not only saves you from getting your pulse up, but it also encourages you to be kind. Kindness moves from one person to another, and it is contagious. By small acts of kindness, you positively impact someone else who in turn is more obliged to do the same for the next person.

Research[8] shows that an act of kindness is contagious and triggers the next person to pay it forward. One single act of generosity could spread three degrees of separation. This means that your single act of kindness could benefit hundreds of people. You become a role model and achieve a greater impact than you imagine.

Being Kind Makes Us Happier

People who are kind are more likely to have healthy and close social connections and relationships. The longest-running study on happiness "A Harvard Study of Adult[9] Development" [10] found a strong association between happiness and close relationships like spouses, family, friends, and social circles. Thus, kindness improves and strengthens social connections and relationships which in turn affects happiness.

Research[11] has also found that those who regularly practice kindness report lower levels of the stress hormone cortisol. This in turn decreases stress and lowers blood pressure. And to top it off a study from the University of California, Berkeley[12] showed that kindness leads to a longer life. Elderly people who regularly volunteered were 44% less likely to die over a five-year period. Even more remarkable is that those who volunteered for two or more organizations had a 63% lower mortality than non-volunteers. This was a stronger factor than exercising four times a week.

Scientific research proves that when we're kind to others, we're rewarded with boosts of dopamine, the neurochemical found in the brain that's linked to pleasure and reward. When dopamine is produced, we experience a big surge of positive feelings that often mimic those of a morphine high. In the realm of giving, this is often referred to as the "Helper's High".

So, despite benefiting people around you, there are also many personal benefits to being kind. Stress is reduced, your career can take off, and you might live longer. Sharing vulnerability and kindness makes you feel better and gives you a sense of belonging. Hold open a door, show courtesy and be thoughtful, and start your own ripples for a contagious kindness.

INSPIRATION - KINDNESS

PERSONAL STORY - AUTHOR ELIN WIBELL

Volunteering at Hriphi Community School in Kuala Lumpur, Malaysia with Myanmar Refugees

When I volunteered to teach science to a class of 8-year old's, I had a feeling that I probably benefited more from the experience, than the children I helped.

I had just moved to Kuala Lumpur, Malaysia, and I had just started my company, Social Good Agency in search of meaningful business and projects. At a dinner party, I started to chat with a woman who told me that Kuala Lumpur had been flooded by refugees from Myanmar. Since they were illegal refugees in Malaysia, they were not allowed to attend school, so a group of dedicated people was teaching pro-bono in an abandoned building in the community.

Now they were looking for a volunteer teacher for grade 3 in Science. My agency was not occupying me full time, so I decided to give it a go. Science had always been my worst subject, but hey, how hard could it be? They were seven- to ten-year-old kids.

Walking into the neighborhood I started to regret my decision, wondering if this was really safe. Kuala Lumpur is a quite dangerous city, and you should have respect for certain areas. But upon reaching the blue shabby building, I was greeted by a group of smiling super cute kids who referred to me as "teacher".

I laughed to myself and wished my old science teacher could see me now. He would have been horrified. The classroom was quite dirty and the material scarce, but it was such a joy to interact with the kids. They were both fun and cool, and we had a lot of laughs. They also told their stories of having to walk with their families from Myanmar to Malaysia to escape the prosecution. A route of 2,632 km, passing through Thailand, at least one full month of walking, probably more. Imagine that...

This was a tough crowd to please. Trust me, if you were not interesting enough, the attention was elsewhere in ten seconds. I always had to structure the class with a back-up plan. In case my class projects wouldn't work if they were totally disinterested, or if the projects were too hard or too easy.

Despite being a professional in the field of communication, this was probably the hardest crowd I ever had to please.

The point of this story was not that I was doing something good. In hindsight, my sessions were probably more beneficial to me than to the kids. Despite having a good time, I could practice public speaking and the need to be interesting at all times. I also felt a sense of joy every Tuesday, unaware of the fact that a nice deed releases hormones and reduces stress. I truly encourage everyone to try one act of kindness per day or week.

"Doing something good did something good to me."

GOING FROM SURVIVING
TO THRIVING

To fully enjoy life, you have to step out of the surviving mode and into the thriving mode. To thrive you are not only keeping your nose above water, you are actually enjoying life.

Unfortunately, the majority of people are stuck in a survival mood. A mood that is catered for a fight or flight situation. A situation where you are trying to cope with all the attacks or problems coming your way. This is obviously not a good mood to be in. It creates anxiety and stress. In this situation, you are actually not thinking constructively either. You are busy searching for reaffirmation on how to handle the problem whether it be to quit your job (flight) or confronting your boss (fight).

This might be easier said than done, but the fact is that you have already done much of the hard work having finished your personal purpose. Remember Aristotle and his theory that the meaning of life is based on the notion that each person's life has a purpose and that the function of one's life is to attain that purpose[13]?

By staying purpose-driven you are closer to self-fulfillment and your life achieves more meaning. The definition of happiness is that it comes when you feel satisfied and fulfilled. When your life fulfills your needs. These needs are now covered in your Personal Purpose. If the purpose doesn't apply to you anymore, tweak it.

Self-fulfillment:

The fulfilment of one's hopes and ambitions.

"It is the striving for self-fulfillment which guides and gives consistency to our lives."
- Wikipedia

You have your personal purpose drafted and the plan to achieve it. Thriving is about mindset, attitude and having a clear goal. Remember, stick to your purpose. When you have a game plan even in the darkest moments, you know you are working towards your goal and it can help cheer you up.

Live Life to The Fullest According to Your Personal Purpose

Another way to fully enjoy life requires you to adopt a mindset and to find yourself in situations that actually provide you with more enthusiasm, happiness, and energy. Once you have found that, focus more on those things and at the same time figure out the situations that take your energy and spend less time on those. We know that this sounds very basic, but the majority of people don't take time to actually analyze those things.

When you are in a thriving mood you are energized. You are living your passion and therefore enjoying the process. It's so important to appreciate this journey, the learnings from failure and the discussions it brings. The problems that will occur on your way are much easier to handle if you are thriving. They are not threats, but learnings and information to get you on the right path. Problems are going to come your way, that is inevitable, but see them as passing hurdles.

BE A POSITIVE FORCE

If you are someone who looks at the world with positive eyes, and encourages people around you, you are someone who other people want to have around. This goes for personal relationships, but it also pertains to the office as well. You would much rather work with someone in a project who you have fun with and who is a positive force, without compromising making the hard decisions and being honest.

So do try to look at life and your surroundings with a positive attitude. Be kind to people and don't assume the worst. Remember the learnings from "Carrying Your Weather" and make an active decision about how you want to approach life.

Throughout life surround yourself with people who are good for you. People who enable you, make you feel good and inspire you. Kind people who lift you up in times of need. Value these people and remember that the same goes for you. Don't forget to be a person who inspires and supports others.

"The Purpose of our lives is to be happy."
- Dalai Lama

Be brave enough to seize opportunities and say "yes" a lot. You will be surprised how much fun you will have and how life will take you into exciting opportunities. By exploring your boundaries, you are able to widen your perspective. You will make new friends and experience more. You will also grow as a person. By daring to do something different, you will be less scared of opportunities. By being open-minded, you will seize unlimited opportunities that might never be expected. Something that is true about the Universe is that when you lift one stone, other changes start to happen to you.

 ## ALWAYS REMEMBER

✓ Be kind to yourself. You are allowed to make mistakes and you will definitely make some. See those as learnings and get rid of the idea of perfection. There is no such thing. By failing we learn, and in a worst-case scenario, you might just:

- Go back with a changed perspective closer to your true purpose

- Have practiced bravery which has made you less scared of other opportunities

- Grown as an individual with a new language, culture, friends, and experiences

- Taken things more lightly

- Realized that things are not as difficult as you once thought

- Improved a positive attitude and your life knowledge

- Strengthen yourself to go out in the world and to embrace what is different

✓ If you have fun and enjoy what you do, others will too. Everyone prefers to work with someone who is in a good place. Enjoy accepting yourself and the freedom of being authentic.

✓ Look at the bright side of life and please remind yourself not to victimize. By being 100 % responsible for your life, it becomes more fun. It is so easy to fall into the old habit of thinking that this only happens to you and that it is unfair. Try to learn from it and see it from a positive angle. This is something you can practice throughout life and something which will make life much easier for you. Also, don't forget to practice gratitude.

"He who risks and fails is better
than he who decides to do nothing."

✓ Dare to dream, have faith in yourself and your abilities. Easier said than done, I know but this is also something you can practice. Practice giving yourself credit when you know you have achieved something. Celebrate the hurdles you overcome and the visions you fulfill.

✓ Enjoy the journey. Enjoy all the small steps you are doing to get closer to your personal purpose. Let it comfort you when in doubt. Step by step you are achieving the higher vision you have set out for yourself. The road might take you on a detour that was not exactly envisioned, but often this initial vision is based on preconceived ideas.

 LIST YOUR UNIQUE ADVANTAGES AND STRENGTHS

Put down some of the advantages and strengths you have, examples:
- Education

- A special talent or skill

- Some saved money or potential revenue streams

- Strong network

- Personality

- Ability to work remotely or a flexible work schedule

- Good friends and support

- Curiosity and eagerness to learn

- Hard-working and determination

- Visionary

1.	
2.	
3.	
4.	
5.	
6.	
7.	
8.	
9.	
10.	

AFTERWORD

Life is a journey and you alone must go through life's teachings. We all have to make our own mistakes and learnings, and there is no template that fits all, nor are there quick fixes.

However, there is no reason why you shouldn't have a game plan.

We hope that your personal purpose will serve as a compass to guide you out of your comfort zone and closer to yourself.

Our goal was to create an inspiring and hopeful book. We hope that you feel inspired and that your energy and drafted personal purpose will give you comfort, joy, and meaning.

A personal purpose isn't a luxury available to only a lucky few. You can tweak some aspects of your life quite easily.

You don't have to change the world, but maybe you will. Regardless of the scope of your personal purpose, enjoy the journey. Live close to yourself and make sure that your current life is aligned with your inner dreams.

We would like to thank everyone who, with enthusiasm, shared their story with the passion to inspire others. Don't forget to upload your own personal purpose on www.queenbeecolony.com to inspire someone else. Kindness is contagious.

Thank you for paying it forward:

Annie Seel

Sarah Belal

Nina and Joe Howden

Ilja Stenberg

Kenneth Andersson

Amanda Wallin

Majka Paulsen Stenberg

Rebecka af Petersens

Abhijit Chatterjee

Josefine Åkerberg

Julie Dobiecki

Christine Knutsson

Jonas Vibell

Samantha Worthington

Photo by Christine Knutsson

ENDNOTES

1   Metz, Thaddeus, "The Meaning of Life", *The Stanford Encyclopedia of Philosophy* (Spring 2021 Edition), Edward N. Zalta (ed.), <https://plato.stanford.edu/archives/spr2021/entries/life-meaning/>.

2   Steinberg, L., & Monahan, K. C. (2007). "Age differences in resistance to peer influence". *Developmental Psychology*, 43(6), 1531–1543. <https://doi.org/10.1037/0012-1649.43.6.1531>.

3   Deloitte Study (2014)"Massive Open Online Courses (MOOCs)": "Not disrupted Yet. But the Future Looks Bright," in 2003. <https://www2.deloitte.com/content/dam/Deloitte/au/Documents/technology-media-telecommunications/deloitte-au-tmt-massive-open-online-courses-011014.pdf>

4   Graham, John "The Importance of Vision" *Life on the Edge*. <https://www.johngraham.org/coach/5-the-importance-of-vision>

5   Aarons-Mele, Morra (May 2020) *Harvard Business Review* "Managing in an Anxious World" <https://hbr.org/cover-story/2020/05/leading-through-anxiety>.

6   University of California - San Diego. "Acts of kindness spread surprisingly easily: just a few people can make a difference." *ScienceDaily*, (10 March 2010). <www.sciencedaily.com/releases/2010/03/100308151049.htm>.

7   Mineo, Liz. *The Harvard Gazette* "Good genes are nice, but joy is better" (April 11, 2017). <https://news.harvard.edu/gazette/story/2017/04/over-nearly-80-years-harvard-study-has-been-showing-how-to-live-a-healthy-and-happy-life/>.

8   Solan, Matthew. "The secret to happiness? Here's some advice from the longest-running study on happiness", *Harvard Health Blog* (October 05, 2017).
<https://www.health.harvard.edu/blog/the-secret-to-happiness-heres-some-advice-from-the-longest-running-study-on-happiness-2017100512543>.

9   "Science of Kindness" *The Random Acts of Kindness Foundation* (April 2021)
<https://www.randomactsofkindness.org/the-science-of-kindness>.

10   Oman, Doug & Thoresen, Carl & Mcmahon, Kay. (1999). Volunteerism and Mortality among the Community-dwelling Elderly. Journal of health psychology. 4. 301-16. 10.1177/135910539900400301.
<https://www.researchgate.net/publication/51736961_Volunteerism_and_Mortality_among_the_Community-dwelling_Elderly>.

11   Metz, Thaddeus, "The Meaning of Life", *The Stanford Encyclopedia of Philosophy* (Spring 2021 Edition), Edward N. Zalta (ed.), <https://plato.stanford.edu/archives/spr2021/entries/life-meaning/>.

12   "Freelancing in America Survey", *Freelancers Union and Upwork* (2017)
<https://www.slideshare.net/upwork/freelancing-in-america-2017/1>.

13   McKinsey Global Institute survey, Independent work: "Choice, necessity, and the gig economy", *McKinsey & Company* (2016) <https://www.mckinsey.com/featured-insights/employment-and-growth/independent-work-choice-necessity-and-the-gig-economy>.

14. Model Illustrations designed by Zuhaibnaqi, a freelance consultant @ Fiverr.

CPSIA information can be obtained
at www.ICGtesting.com
Printed in the USA
BVHW092346170223
658738BV00003B/311